CODEPENDENCE

AND THE POWER OF

DETACHMENT

ALSO BY KAREN CASEY

CODEPENDENCE

AND THE POWER OF

DETACHMENT

How To Set Boundaries and
Make Your Life Your Own

KAREN CASEY

Conari Press

Cover Design: Carmen Fortunato
Layout Design: 📖 *the*BookDesigners | *bookdesigners.com.*

For permission requests, please contact the publisher at:
Mango Publishing Group
2850 S Douglas Road, 4th Floor
Coral Gables, FL 33134 USA
info@mango.bz

For special orders, quantity sales, course adoptions and corporate sales, please email the publisher at sales@mango.bz. For trade and wholesale sales, please contact Ingram Publisher Services at customer.service@ingramcontent.com or +1.800.509.4887.

Codependence and the Power of Detachment: How to Set Boundaries and Make Your Life Your Own

Library of Congress Cataloging-in-Publication number: 2021951255
ISBN: (print) 978-1-64250-445-3 (ebook) 978-1-64250-446-0
BISAC category code: SEL003000, SELF-HELP / Adult Children of Substance Abusers

Printed in the United States of America

CONTENTS

CONTENTS

"We can take charge of our own lives, not the lives of other people."
—*A Life of My Own*

PREFACE

T HE CONCEPT OF DETACHMENT is one I have reckoned with
for more years than I care to count. I had no idea as a youngster
that my constant fear, which manifested as daily stomachaches and
frequent vomiting, was due to my inability to detach from the scowls
or scoldings, real or imagined, I frequently got from my parents. From
a very young age, I was a master at reading the facial expressions and
body language of other people. I needed to know how someone else
was feeling in order to know if I was acceptable, loved, worthwhile, or
at fault for their bad mood. I lived in fear of frowns and scolding when
I was small. Not looking at other people around me would have meant
I had no idea who I was or what I needed to do.

I didn't know if other kids my age ever felt like I felt. I was too
afraid to ask them. I wasn't even able to ask my three siblings how
they felt about the tension in our home. I simply remember that we

all remained quiet and escaped to the bedroom when my dad got mad, which was soon after he got home from work most evenings.

Anger was, without a doubt, the prevalent emotion in our house. My father's expression of it was frequent and loud, and it scared me. I used to watch my mother to see if she felt the same fear that I did. She generally looked down or away when he ranted. Sometimes she went to the bathroom and cried. She seldom confronted my father's anger. But when she did, his rage only worsened. I used to be afraid friends would come over or call while he was yelling. I didn't want them to hear him curse so vehemently. I thought they might tell their parents, whom I had seldom heard curse, and they wouldn't be able to come to my house anymore.

There didn't seem to be any one thing that made my father mad. Minor infractions—like one of us leaving his evening paper in a disorganized pile or forgetting a bike in the driveway—resulted in major outbursts and spankings. My father wasn't always physically abusive while angry, but my brother and I did feel the pain of his hand often enough.

My siblings and I carried the emotional scars of our childhood into our other relationships as we got older because we didn't know any other way of functioning. Our scars manifested in obvious, though very different, ways. My oldest sister developed panic attacks. Sister number two has struggled with being overweight for most of her adult life. My brother had a full-blown nervous breakdown in his early twenties. He has been emotionally stuck in an unchallenging career ever since. I think I am the lucky one. I turned to alcohol and drugs and men to mask the pain of supposed unworthiness, and I eventually got the emotional and spiritual help I needed through the fellowship of Alcoholics Anonymous (AA) and Al-Anon.

Gathering the information to write this book has been an intensely absorbing undertaking. I had not thought a great deal about my own childhood for a number of years. Through a series of efforts, thousands of Twelve Step meetings, hundred of sessions with sponsors, hours and hours of prayer and meditation, and my willingness to see the past in a different light, I have finally been able to leave it behind. However, to do justice to the topic of detachment, I needed to recall "what it was like, what happened, and what it's like now," as we say in AA meetings. And I can say with absolute resolve that I will not choose to repeat the pain of my past.

I have learned how to make a different choice when I am tempted to let the behavior of others determine what my next act will be. I hope that what I share in this book will help you understand that you, too, can make a different choice if you find yourself repeatedly caught in unproductive, unrewarding, unloving exchanges with the significant people in your life.

INTRODUCTION

I STILL VIVIDLY recall when I first read *Why Am I Afraid to Tell You Who I Am?* by John Powell. When I got to page thirty-eight, I was stunned to read a description of my most common response to the behavior of the significant people in my life. Powell was walking down a New York City street with his journalist friend, Sidney Harris. They stopped at a newspaper vendor's shack to pick up the morning edition. The vendor was an extremely unpleasant man who not only ignored Harris when he said good morning, but also didn't thank him when Harris told him to keep the change. Powell immediately asked his friend why he was so kind and generous to such an ungrateful, mean-spirited individual. Harris replied, "Why should I let him decide what kind of day I am going to have?"

I realized at that moment that I had spent my entire life letting the actions or words or mere glances of others trigger my behavior, my feelings, my attitude, my self-assessment, and thus my plan for each day, as well as my imagined future. And I had never realized it. It simply had not occurred to me that I could or should be the one to decide exactly who I would bring to the party every day of my life.

How others act does not need to affect how we think or act. There are countless situations and people we have no control over. A friend's angry outburst, a motorist's failure to see our car in a busy intersection, a spouse's relapse into alcohol or drug use—all of these things may upset us. But that upset can be brief if we keep the power over our own feelings.

There is a difference between letting the reactions of others take over our life and respecting others' opinions while maintaining our own perspective and integrity. Failing to understand that difference creates the inner chaos that keeps many of us stuck in old, unproductive behavior and filled with uncertainty and anxiety. Letting someone else decide who we will be, how we will act, and what we will feel implies that we have given up our own life in exchange for whatever the other person wants us to be. When we adopt opinions that aren't consistent with our personal values, we are not living our own lives. We are not free.

Coming to understand and eventually celebrate our powerlessness over people, places, and things is the key to our freedom—freedom from enmeshment, freedom from the fear of rejection, freedom from the fear of failure, freedom from the fear of success. We are blessed, every one of us, with gifts that are needed by others who are traveling this path with us. But until we are free to see who we really are, we will not be able to recognize that which we have been created to give. And until we can care deeply for others from a more objective perspective, we will not be able to give our special gifts to the world around us.

The women and men you will get to know throughout this book will offer you glimpses of the trauma of attachment, more generally labeled codependency. Codependency isn't a twentieth-century phenomenon, but in the last quarter of that century, we began to recognize this form of dependence on others as a malady of sorts. Fortunately it is now being discussed in therapy sessions, Twelve Step meetings, and books galore.

The opposite of the unhealthy attachment of codependency is detachment. Detachment is the ability to care deeply about a situation or another person from an objective point of view. We are able to care but not be controlled by or invested in how another person responds to us.

Healthy detachment wears many identities. Letting others take care of their own affairs and not doing for others what they need to do for themselves is detachment. Not creating or preventing a crisis when it's clearly not our business to be involved is detachment. Not manipulating others to carry out some aspect of their lives according to our wishes rather than according to their own plan is detachment. It is neither kind nor unkind to be detached. It is simply being in charge of the only things we need to be in charge of.

Newcomers often think that disinterest is detachment, and sometimes disinterest is the only way they can begin the real process of detachment. I could not get my mind around the concept of detachment when I first heard it. But choosing to be uninterested in what someone else was doing, or, for me, even feigning disinterest, was a beginning. Up until that point, I had no idea how to move my focus away from any person who was significant in my life at that moment.

Detachment is a concept that I and many other people struggle with. Far too many of us grew up in households that couldn't prepare us to know ourselves as competent, worthy people because our caregivers—sometimes parents, sometimes older siblings—didn't recognize their own worthiness either. From the women and men I spoke with, I heard hundreds of examples of successful and unsuccessful experiences of detaching from the frequent, real or imagined, negative behavior of others in our lives. From them I also discovered some shortcuts to changing behaviors that are counterproductive to lives of inner peace. And they demonstrated the joy that they have come to know from being able to detach—from their ability to be independent and compassionate, yet no longer clingy and obsessed with getting constant approval from others.

Be assured that this book is not fostering total independence—not by a long shot. We all need others in our lives. Instead, it is about developing a healthy *inter*dependence—that is, independence that frees all of us to be all we can be, but still allows us to get an appropriate amount of support and encouragement from other travelers.

All the stories in this book have one thing in common: there is now peace where before there was pain. There is now willingness to turn the other cheek rather than insisting on being right. Detachment isn't rocket science. It isn't beyond anyone's understanding. All it takes to change how we see our lives, how we live our lives, how we envision our lives for the future, is a willingness to look at the possibilities.

I

FROM ENMESHMENT TO FREEDOM

MY STORY

WHEN WE'RE CAUGHT in the pain of enmeshment, we don't know who we are, what we think or want, or what direction is right for us to move in. We have traded in our own identity for the identity we think another person prefers. And when we have many significant people in our lives who we assume we need to satisfy, we necessarily develop many personalities. Chaos reigns, at least in our own minds, when we are living for and through other people.

That's how I lived life for my first thirty-six years. I vividly remember standing in our kitchen and crying after my first husband, Bill, and I separated, because I had no idea what I wanted to fix for my dinner. I had spent twelve years cooking whatever he wanted, and the sad part was that it had not occurred to me that it could have been different. It wasn't because he was abusive and demanded that I cook his favorite things; I had simply lived my life around him in every regard. I remember feeling as though I were on the hot seat whenever he asked me what I thought about a book we had both read, a movie we had recently seen, a philosophical idea he had painstakingly explained to me, or even something as simple as the weather. I would nervously search my mind to guess what he might be thinking about the topic so my answer could match, or at least complement, his ideas. I feared his look of boredom whenever I offered what he considered an obviously uninformed answer.

Did he really look at me this way? Probably not. Did he demand that I pay him this homage? Of course not. It was simply what I had learned to do in relationships in order to avoid being rejected. But in the end, my pandering could not keep him in the relationship. And it had given me no happiness either.

My experience with Bill was not the first relationship I had tried to control by seeking to make myself indispensable. With my first boyfriend in high school, I had behaved similarly. If Steve was moody, I was the reason. I needed to be more exciting perhaps. If he didn't call when I expected him to, I was certain a breakup was imminent. If he had not asked me for a specific weekend date, I knew it was because he was waiting for a better date to surface. I lived my life around his every mood and meager offerings of attention. I watched him like a hawk to assess how I was doing in my role as girlfriend.

My early relationships illustrate the too-common behaviors of the enmeshed, attached, codependent person. My identity was clearly an extension of the partner I was with. If he turned away, I felt invisible. If he praised me or focused attention on me in any way, it suggested I mattered. I was continuously afraid that every relationship partner and friend would eventually reject me unless I was the perfect counterpart to his or her identity. Mine was an impossible assignment. My inner turmoil and overwhelming self-doubt only increased in magnitude.

Considering myself a whole person, worthy to be valued solely on my own terms, was beyond my comprehension. While growing up, I had not received the kind of perspective from my family that would have helped me develop a positive self-image. Being constantly available and ingratiating was the only way I knew to get the feedback I craved. At the end of my relationships with Steve and Bill, I was aware that the behavior I had tried to master could not prevent rejection. But I had no other behavior to resort to. I didn't even realize it could be different.

My reliance on open expressions of love from significant other people in my life was absolute for a number of years. I didn't really appreciate the depth of my own dependence on others' approval until I had been sober and in Alcoholics Anonymous (AA) for a while. It wasn't that I didn't see how much I wanted to be noticed and liked—I had just never acknowledged how anxious I felt when the attention I sought was not forthcoming.

But while I assumed that AA was going to change all of the behaviors, perceptions and assumptions that had haunted me for years and fed my self-doubt, toward the end of my first year of recovery, I was closer to suicide than at any time previously in my life. I had considered suicide the perfect out for many years; however, I had never planned it in as much detail as I did after about twelve months of sobriety. Stacked on my kitchen table were the towels I planned to stuff around the windows of my apartment. All I needed to do was tightly tuck them next to the sills and turn on the gas from the stove. I felt numb and yet relieved that the pain would soon be gone.

Then there was a rapid, persistent knocking at the door.

I wasn't expecting anyone and considered not answering, but a voice began calling my name. It sounded quite impatient, so I eventually opened the door. My visitor, a woman I barely recognized, insisted we had made an appointment to discuss financial planning. She brushed right past me and walked into my kitchen.

After a good bit of probing on her part, I told her about my overwhelming fear and depression, although not my planned suicide. She said she understood, had experienced this form of anxiety herself, gave it a name, and told me I was on the threshold of a great spiritual awakening. She said that my experience was simply a point on the continuum of spiritual growth and that most individuals who were seeking a deeper, better understanding of their purpose in life, as I had been, went through this phase.

Something inside me told me she was right. I could feel a change throughout my body as she spoke. A calm settled over me. I had not felt calm for many weeks. I had the quiet but profound knowledge that I hadn't ever needed to discuss finances with her. But I had needed to speak to someone about my crippling fears. Within a few minutes of her mysterious presence in my home, I was freed from the need to end my life. She left almost as quickly as she had come, but she was, without a doubt, God-sent.

|▙▟▙▟▙|

STILL ADDICTED TO APPROVAL

One might think that following this profound couple of hours with the mysterious "financial planner," I would never have experienced fear again. While it's true that the overwhelming, free-floating kind of fear was gone, I still sought concrete evidence of approval from most of the significant people in my life. I still feared what others were thinking.

In the third year of my sobriety and following the completion of my PhD, I took a job that I was not well prepared for and had a boss who was demanding and demeaning. My well-worn habit of making another person my "god" was accelerated on that job. Having lived that way since childhood and having never really freed myself of the need to please others at any cost, I found that with a boss such as mine, all of my old responses were easily triggered. I was addicted to approval, period!

I also began to understand my need for control—control over what another person was thinking about me. It was a constant need in nearly every relationship in my life, as much as I did not want to admit it. As diligently as I tried, I continued to scan the expressions of others, particularly the expressions of my boss and my significant other, for my "control fix." Getting the fix one needs in order to continue living from one minute to the next, whether from a drug or from the praise of a person, is a debilitating way to live. I wouldn't say that the addiction of codependency is more harmful than addiction to alcohol or other mood-altering chemicals, but I can't say that it is less harmful either.

Eventually the pain of my work environment and my boss's behavior sent me into outpatient treatment for codependency, and I hurried back to Al-Anon, the program I had sought help from before I got sober myself. I had begun my journey in Al-Anon in 1975, as a desperate measure to try to change the drinking pattern of the significant person in my life. I didn't glean from that first meeting that Al-Anon wasn't created for that purpose. In fact, I came home with an Al-Anon book and eagerly read it from cover to cover. At the next meeting, when asked how I was doing, I said that I was fine—I had finished the book! The other group members laughed and suggested I begin reading again, this time reading only the page for the day. The book's title, *One Day at a Time in Al-Anon*, had not even registered when I picked it up that first night.

What I had not yet fully understood was that I had only a moment-by-moment reprieve from codependent feelings, and these moments were the direct result of my willingness to look only to my Higher Power for my good feelings. I am so grateful to have been introduced to the concept of a Higher Power in Al-Anon. It relaxed me to envelop myself in the comfort of "a god" as I understood him, a comfort that was always there when the comfort from a partner might not be.

THE LEARNING CURVE

Seeking approval from others for my very existence was such an ingrained habit that knowing I didn't need approval was beyond my comprehension for a long time. Fortunately, my sponsor reminded me often that I was on a learning curve and that I was right where I needed to be. Her words of comfort and her wisdom kept me from losing all hope.

Meanwhile, a treatment counselor suggested that when we feel as if we're falling into old patterns of behavior, we should retreat to a safe place for a prayer and an inner pep talk. The bathroom became my haven. I can remember how quickly and frequently I would head for the bathroom to look at myself in the mirror and silently remind myself that God (the God I didn't yet really trust) did love me and that I was worthy with or without acceptance, approval, or love of any particular person.

I can't say exactly when the change began to happen for me. I can only say that it did. I simply noted, on occasion, that I seemed unaffected by harsh words or intentional scowls directed at me by the important people in my life. It wasn't that I no longer cared what others might think; it was that I had begun to feel a new confidence. Was the change because of meetings, daily readings, reaching out to others in new ways, or prayer? Probably it was a result of the combination of all of these. More specifically, my confidence probably developed because I had let go of my shame around the attachment, the enmesh-ment that I felt with so many other people in my life, and I had started discussing the problem in meetings.

I also learned that controlling others so that they provide me with what I think I need to feel good about myself is like travel-ing through a maze that has no exit. I would never find what I am seeking. Grasping the essence of the First Step of the Al-Anon pro-gram—that we are powerless over alcohol and thus powerless over those who suffer from the disease of alcoholism, as well as over all others, too—offered me the first sign of relief, and thus hope, that I can survive within a relationship.

My second experience in Al-Anon has continued to this day. I am convinced that my sobriety owes nearly as much to Al-Anon as to AA. I say this because in my forty-five years of recovery, I have known far too many people who have returned to drinking as the result of painful relationships. Al-Anon has not taken away all the pain in my significant relationships, but it has given me the tools to deal with the issues that surface when people honestly relate to each other.

It is very, very hard to change the only behavior that you're famil-iar with; mind-sets are deeply ingrained. But they can change. I am living proof.

|◆◆◆◆◆|

INSIGHTS

When we are overly attached to the feelings, the opinions, and the action of others, we have no life of our own. We are not emotionally separate and healthy, but enmeshed and unfocused. When we are will-ingly, obsessively encumbered by the emotional presence of the other person, we cannot have clarity about our own lives, and we cannot hear the messages that are trying to reach us about the right path to take or the right decision to make.

Offering attention to others is not a bad thing. But there is a significant difference between offering loving attention to someone in need and totally giving up attention to one's own needs in the process. Nobody is helped by our obsession with others. While it is neither right nor helpful to isolate ourselves from the people who happen upon our path, learning from them comes as the result of healthy interaction, not obsessive, compulsive attention.

The value of detachment is that it frees both persons who are caught in the web of obsessive attention and attachment. Detachment doesn't mean a sudden decision to ignore a loved one. Rather, it means lovingly moving our attention away from them. It means looking about our life fully and appreciatively, not narrowly, as we are wont to do when we have captured a hostage by means of attachment.

DETACHMENT IN ACTION

JEAN'S STORY

I FIRST BECAME ACQUAINTED with Jean in an Al-Anon meeting. It was a large group of men and women, and it was the custom of this particular group to stay together as one unit throughout discussion, so I never spoke to her individually until I happened to sit next to her at one of the noon meetings. Instantly I could tell she had the kind of program—i.e., a gentle way of living—all Al-Anon-goers seek. I was curious about her history and told her so. I also wondered what happened to her, because Jean's glow told me what life was like for her now.

We met for lunch, and she gave me the short story on how she had come to Al-Anon. Jean was the middle daughter in a middle-class "functional" family, twice divorced, and the mother of two boys. She had been an artist, making her living in the arts for more than twenty-five years in Vermont. Because of a change in her personal life, she gravitated to her present home and the city where I met her.

"I knew years ago that I wanted to be on a spiritual journey," she said. "[T]he universe sent me an alcoholic, and the journey began."

Like so many of us, Jean had gotten romantically involved with a charming, fun-loving man who turned out to be an alcoholic. He followed her to Florida, where they shared a vacation condo for a time, and the cycle of pain and chaos began. He got sober, then relapsed—again and again. She propped him up for a while, expecting the next round of sober days to last forever. Eventually he moved on, but before that time, she was guided toward Al-Anon.

STEPPING BACK

One of the first things Jean said to me was that before Al-Anon, she felt she was on a "brain train," trying to analyze and control every event and outcome. She is aware that for many years, men had been projects for her. When she couldn't change the man, she would change herself to make the two of them appear more compatible as a couple. That habit rings true for many of us in Al-Anon. It's one of the classic symptoms of our disease. No matter what circumstance we find ourselves in, we will try to change it or us to provide the outcome we think we deserve.

One of the things Jean learned in Al-Anon was detachment, which she describes as "stepping back and leaving room for God to do God's work." Detachment can mean stepping back not only from people, but also from places, things, or activities. Jean shared that she had never known contentment until she decided to quit doing many of the activities that had consumed her time for years.

Jean has attained balance in her life now—balance coupled with a peacefulness that radiates from her. She now works as a personal chef for an elderly couple, and she loves the quiet rhythm of her life. Her creativity has continued to blossom; she simply exhibits it in new ways, such as in how she cares for the couple, how she prepares meals for them, and how she is nurturing them on the final phase of their life's journey. Caring for others deeply from an objective stance—which is, of course, one way to define detachment—is what she is constantly practicing.

INSIGHTS

Jean's image of stepping back is a great one to conjure up during those moments when we're tempted to take charge of a person or an experience that is clearly in God's domain. Stepping back allows us to let God take ownership of the solution. Deciding to leave the situation in God's hands rather than trying to change it ourselves offers us the same relief that we ask for in the Serenity Prayer: "God grant me the serenity to accept the things I cannot change."

One of the best reasons for stepping back or detaching from a person, place, or thing is, as Jean discovered, the quiet contentment that almost immediately comes over us. Our minds cannot be on two things at the same time. No matter how organized we are or how much of a perfectionist we want to be, our minds cannot handle more than one thought in any single moment. When we try to cram in more than one, our anxiety level rises. Thinking only one thought at a time, and then occasionally getting really quiet between thoughts, will profoundly change how we experience life. We may need to remember to step back many times a day, even many times an hour, but the payoff is worth it.

Another idea that Jean shared is that "there are at least twenty or more ways to solve every problem." She said that this knowledge is what gives her the assurance to step back. She learned that nothing must be handled immediately. In fact, the best way to proceed in almost every instance is to wait awhile, pray and meditate a bit, seek the inner quiet, and then trust the urging that comes from that place of knowing.

AN ACQUIRED HABIT

ROSE'S STORY

ROSE, THE MOTHER OF NINE, had an alcoholic husband. Even though he had exhibited signs of the illness even in his youth, she knew nothing about it when they married. He wasn't physically abusive, but he was emotionally abusive, as well as emotionally absent. He was seldom around to help with the chores or the discipline when the demands of so many children overwhelmed her. Alone, she shouldered the responsibility of the children on a day-to-day basis. For many years she struggled, not always in silence, but with no resolution. She assumed that if she did things differently in their home, his behavior would change.

Then she read about Al-Anon in her church bulletin. For many weeks in a row, she noted the day and the time of the meeting. She wondered whether or not it could help her, but she was scared to go or to ask more questions about it.

Finally, at the urging of a friend in whom Rose had confided, she worked up her courage and went to an Al-Anon meeting. At first she didn't dare let anyone know she was there because of her husband. He was well known in the church community, and she didn't want to ruin his reputation. He would definitely have gotten mad if he found out she had revealed anything about him or their home life to people in their community. Then, after a few weeks of listening and watching, she tentatively began to share some of her experiences and listen to the wisdom of others.

But her vision was still blurred for a number of years. Her husband finally went to treatment, but not much changed in their lives. He didn't stay sober, the children didn't calm down, and Rose didn't successfully detach. For many years Rose didn't feel successful as a mother and wife because of the way her children and husband behaved. But to simply detach, to draw a boundary around herself and believe that "what they do is not a reflection on me," wasn't possible for her right away.

Another challenge was that she had been raised to think it was her job to take care of others, children as well as husbands. Letting them take care of themselves was against her grain. Caretaking was a key part of her identity. If she were to let them take care of themselves, what would she do with her time? She was afraid she would feel irrelevant to her family.

A NEW PERSPECTIVE

Learning to live in her own space without letting the behaviors of others trouble her was far more elusive than Rose had ever imagined.

But after her husband's unsuccessful treatment experience, she had embarked on a lifelong quest to see her own life from a new perspective. Rose did not walk away from the help that was available through the meetings of Al-Anon, and for many years she never missed a weekly meeting.

Eventually, Rose learned that she could live with her husband's alcoholism without being constantly controlled by it or any of the behavior it triggered. She phrased this understanding in a poignant way: "I learned to walk next to the disease without letting it affect me in a harmful way." She began to understand that she could more peacefully live with the active alcoholism in her home. On many days she was aware that she was actually free of her obsession with her husband's drinking.

After she had garnered years of wisdom and strength from her contemporaries in Al-Anon, Rose eventually learned to detach. By the time the disease of alcoholism reared its ugly head among a number of her children, she was able to observe it, not make such a big deal of it, and let the process of the disease and the hoped-for recovery take its own course. She had learned from Al-Anon that she could love her husband and stay with him even though he was not sober, so she felt quite empowered to let her children find their own path to recovery.

Fortunately, each of them did.

![decorative divider]

INSIGHTS

One thing Rose had going for her was that her commitment to her own growth was an absolute. By being truly invested in seeking help and listening to the wisdom of others, she discovered the courage to make changes in her own behavior.

Detachment is a decision, first and foremost. We can choose to be martyrs. We can choose to be blamers. We can choose to be rueful or full of self-pity. Many of us in Al-Anon made one of these choices, or all three, before seeking help in the fellowship of the program. However, like Rose, we can choose new perceptions; we can learn new behaviors, and we can make new decisions about how to live our lives, whom to include in our lives, and what our destination will be. But we cannot move forward without first making the conscious decision to do something different.

One of the coping tools Rose's years in Al-Anon has given her is the courage to physically remove herself from her home situation when she needs to. At one point she had to leave her home for a number of months in order to preserve her sanity and feel any sense of well-being. It was an extremely difficult decision, and she didn't get much support from her grown children or the extended family. But she knew leaving for a while was the only way to move forward in her own life. She said the separation from her husband did scare her, but she felt her Higher Power within encouraging her to make the move, and that Higher Power sustained her throughout her months away from home.

She returned, as she always knew she would, but she returned stronger, more positively detached than before and able to fully love and support her husband as he was. And she knew she would never need to leave for that long again. She knew that it didn't matter how he closed out the remaining years of his life; she was able to live hers with the support of her friends in Al-Anon, the tools she had acquired in the groups, and the realization that wherever she was, her Higher Power was present to empower her to do the next right thing.

In our discussion, Rose noted how applicable the principle of detachment was in every emotionally charged situation, not just those times when one of her alcoholic "qualifiers" got her attention. Our qualifiers, those men and women over whom we obsess, demand a lot from us. There are many ways we can behave differently with not only our partners and family members, but also our coworkers, our friends, our neighbors, even those strangers who get our attention many times daily. None of us goes through a single day free of opportunities to overreact to situations that really need not affect us. That means every day offers us many opportunities to practice detachment.

Rose also said it was important for her to distinguish between being negatively passive and making a conscious choice to disengage from a situation that had snagged her emotions. It was and is her inclination to acquiesce, she said. However, she learned the difference between quietly detaching from a situation versus shutting down her feelings. We, too, can learn to be disengaged without being passive. We can learn to take charge of our thoughts, rather than letting our thoughts take us where we don't need to go. Any of these ideas, in fact, will change every aspect of our lives immeasurably.

Finally, from Al-Anon, Rose learned not to do for others what they need to do for themselves. Even though her husband did not stay sober, his disease was his to shoulder. She did not cause it, nor could she cure it. Not doing for others what they need to do for themselves sounds so simple. No doubt many of us think, "Well, I don't do that." But if we are honest and examine our behavior, we may discover that in myriad ways we are picking up the slack or the mess, around our homes or elsewhere, rather than letting the perpetrator take responsibility. For many years, Rose strove to be both mother and father to her children, trying to make up for her husband's lack of participation at home. But her dedication to being a caretaker made her a slave, and it also never gave her husband the opportunity to take responsibility for his part in raising their family. The unfortunate fact is that *every time we take on someone else's responsibility, we are keeping them stuck, and in the process making a hostage of both of us. It is not easy to let the addict mature, but we must. We are harming him or her every time we step in and bring order to the chaos he or she created.*

Whenever we are considering doing something for or on behalf of someone else, we need to make an honest judgment about whether or not it is appropriate. Perhaps we need to allow the other person to learn what taking responsibility really means. Giving up our control does not come easily. We often think that our own lives won't be what they should be if others don't carry out our instructions. For some of us, it is as difficult to make this change as it is for an addict to become more responsible. And it is just as necessary.

Because of what she learned in Al-Anon, Rose now refuses to suffer because of someone else's actions. She knows now that we are never the cause of what someone else chooses to do nor can we control another's choices. The more quickly we acknowledge this fact and change our responses accordingly, the more quickly we will know a semblance of peace in our lives. Just as Rose gradually accepted that her husband's and children's actions were not a reflection of herself or her mothering skills, we, too, can learn to separate our own identities and actions from those of the other people in our lives.

One of the first points Rose and I talked about was whether detachment is simply a decision or a gift from one's Higher Power. We decided it might be either. And either way, Rose said, "Detachment is an acquired habit."

SURRENDER AT LAST

ANNA'S STORY

INTERVIEWING ANNA was a must for me, because I had observed, over the years, a transformation in her very being.

When we first met nearly three decades ago, she was an angry, uncompromising woman. She had been hurt in a previous marriage and was not interested in letting any man, or woman for that matter, get away with behavior or opinions that she didn't agree with. She had to address every point of disagreement. She was the authority, whether she understood the circumstances or not. Because she was European by birth and had a lyrical accent, she managed to charm most of us in spite of her quick dismissal of ideas and opinions that were out of favor with her.

Because of Anna's history with her first husband, it was easy to make excuses for her behavior. She had met Paul while he was in her homeland. He was an attractive, successful, confident physician, and his self-assurance convinced her she would be as well taken care of with him as she had been in her upbringing. She also assumed her marriage would resemble the marriage of her parents. Her mother had married the man who was her "second choice," since marriage to the real love of her life had not worked out. Her marriage to the man who was to be Anna's father was a good one, Anna said. Her father was a wonderful provider and a gentle man, but she felt her mother might have been happier had she married her first paramour. Anna was conscious of not wanting to disappoint her parents, even though she did balk at the family rules on occasion. Marrying Paul seemed to be the right thing to do, because her parents were proud of the prospect of having a son-in-law who was a handsome and respectable physician—and an American.

It wasn't hard to leave her homeland, Anna said. She felt prepared. Her life had been blessed with guidance and a college education, and she had the self-confidence to make this move with a man who seemed to offer a life similar to the one she was leaving behind. She had visited him in America before becoming engaged; she had met his parents and his friends and liked them all. She was eager to create a new beginning for herself, and marriage was the vehicle.

But a surprise was in store for her when she took up residence in America as "the doctor's wife." Very soon she realized she was his trophy. She was cute and had a delightful accent and a European mystique about her. She could see she was Paul's toy to show off to his friends, and as such, she was not expected to have a mind of her own. On the contrary, it wasn't unusual for him to correct her, even belittle her, in front of their guests. Her wish for some independence quickly sent the marriage into a tailspin. Paul needed to be in control, and Anna needed to speak her mind, as she had been allowed to do in her childhood home. In fact, she had been encouraged to develop her own ideas and opinions. To give up this way of being was like giving up her very presence.

Perhaps the marriage would have ended sooner, but Anna gave birth to a daughter, Polly. Polly was the apple of Paul's eye for the first few years of her life, or at least it seemed that way. However, Anna got a different sense of him as a father when she returned to her homeland with Polly to think over their marriage. Upon her return, she discovered that Paul had already moved all their belongings into the attic. It seemed he had not missed the apple of his eye that much, after all.

Soon after Anna came back, Paul said he was through with the marriage. She was devastated, not so much because she had a great love for him but because she didn't know if she could handle life alone in America. She pleaded for him to see a counselor with her, but his mind was made up. It was over. Anna moved into a small duplex, a home far different from what she had grown accustomed to while married to a wealthy physician. But at least there she could speak her mind.

A BARRAGE OF CRITICISMS

Within a few months, Anna met Howie, the man whom she has been with ever since. He was Paul's opposite in every way. He was funny, warm, supportive, and emotional. Anna couldn't believe her good fortune. Howie moved in to help care for Polly after Anna broke her leg. Though his personality was so different from Anna's, he made her laugh, and he adored her. She had gone back to school in order to be able to support herself and Polly, and he praised her efforts constantly. She needed the compliments to keep moving forward.

However, she was soon to realize there were parts of Howie she was not comfortable with. His background had been extremely different from hers. He was of a different faith. His only sibling was a very unstable person. He was estranged from his parents. He was also an addict, albeit recovering, and she had no understanding of this condition. When she heard him share his story at an AA meeting, she was embarrassed for both of them, particularly because of the tears he shed. Unfortunately, she was not able to repay his frequent compliments with kind words. Most of his efforts at work and in his personal life she disparaged. She wasn't clear in her own mind about why she needed to criticize him, but criticize she did. He tried to ignore the constant barrage of "corrections," understanding that they were about her past and not their present, but they were discouraging to him.

One of the main difficulties Anna had was dealing with her feelings of superiority, which made her judgmental toward others. Because she was far less emotional than Howie, she saw his frequent tears as a sign of weakness, thus inferiority. Being vulnerable was simply not an option for Anna. She would never let another person into her life the way she had allowed Paul in. Eventually Anna realized that she was treating Howie as Paul had treated her. To her shock, she saw that she had almost assumed Paul's persona in her relationship with Howie.

Howie wanted Anna to go to Al-Anon. Because she had not been part of his past using days, she saw no need for it. Besides, she was not interested in spirituality, group "therapy," or changing her behavior. Although the principles of the program would have been beneficial not only in her relationship with Howie but also in her relationship with Polly, Anna couldn't be sold on Al-Anon.

Then a personal crisis occurred that was affecting their marriage. Anna was frantic when she called me for solace, and I suggested that she turn to Al-Anon for guidance and support. She finally agreed to try it for a few weeks.

At first, hearing others share so honestly and completely about themselves at Al-Anon made her uncomfortable. She didn't want to know people that well. She went to the weekly meetings because she had made a contract with her sponsor and with Howie, but frequently resisted hearing the message that the meeting might have taught her.

▶️◀️

LETTING GO OF JUDGMENT

What finally happened for Anna is what happens for every person who continues to show up at fellowship meetings: the program will get you whether or not you get the program. She was surprised to discover her thinking beginning to change, in spite of herself. Her judgments became less severe. Her patience increased. She learned to remain quiet even when she desperately wanted to criticize Howie or someone else. Most of all, she learned how her habit of judging others kept her attached to the behavior of everyone around her. She had never seen this attachment as a problem before, considering it her job to notice and pass judgment on everyone who crossed her path. To simply notice people without judging them seemed like a job half completed. She didn't understand that judging others hurt her as much as it did them.

Since developing the habit of detachment, Anna says she and Howie have wonderful conversations. She can feel supportive of him even when he begins to struggle. If she feels some irritation, she has learned to move away from the conversation for a while. Detachment is a habit that she continues to hone, but she is amazed at her willingness to practice it on a regular basis. Many of her actions now were unthinkable not so many years ago.

Because I knew her before her recovery began, I can vouch for how remarkable Anna's change has been. There is a softness about her that was unfathomable three decades ago. The tenderness she shows

Howie and everyone else who crosses her path is sincere. Her superiority is gone. Her judgments are few. Her willingness to believe in a spiritual guide is developing.

She now sees how much more contentment life can hold when she leaves the decisions that need to be made by others to them. Not trying to judge or control anyone but herself has given her a great deal more time to pursue hobbies that she had abandoned. And she has finally been able to address another problem area in her life: her nicotine addiction.

Anna knows her life isn't free of all challenges for all time, but she has grown accustomed to using the tools she has gathered from Twelve Step meetings, daily readings, and myriad conversations she has enjoyed with her sponsor and others. She does not doubt that these new habits will sustain her if she ever finds herself in a troubling time again. She is the first to say that what she eventually was able to share at Al-Anon meetings, coupled with a little willingness to change aspects of her behavior, has given her and Howie a new, refreshed life filled with honesty, mutual emotional support, and hope for their future together.

|ıı⊞ıı|

INSIGHTS

Anna learned to practice the Al-Anon principles without wholeheartedly believing in them at first. She insists that pretending to accept things that were or are anathema to her, as the principles of Al-Anon were to her, makes them acceptable in time. She learned that the mind does not make up the ideas or the conversations without our help; it simply mirrors back our words. Therefore, we can change our minds if we change what we say to them. She experienced such a mind shift just by hearing the principles of Al-Anon and lessons from her fellow members over and over.

Another valuable lesson Anna has learned is to keep quiet, at least occasionally, when she has nothing nice to say. Many of us heard our parents preach this principle when we were young: if you don't have something nice to say, say nothing at all. It's not easy to do, however. As a child I was often told, "Just keep your mouth shut." Of course I couldn't, and I paid many consequences as a result.

Anna was not always successful at living up to this principle for the first couple of years, but she kept trying. Howie was aware of her efforts and was willing to forgive her slips. Now, even though she may still feel the need to respond, she often keeps her responses to herself. Her most frequent, silent response now to the innumerable little irritations of life—particularly those that center on Howie, Polly, or her coworkers—is, "It will be okay." Even though we hear from our program friends and sponsors the value of doing the next right thing, sometimes the next right thing is to do and say nothing. Learning that we are capable of observing an experience with no reaction, or at the very least a silent reaction, is gratifying.

BREAKTHROUGH

BARBARA'S STORY

B ARBARA GREW UP IN A CHAOTIC, alcoholic home, where her father demeaned her and her mother on a regular basis. As a young girl, she always felt sad and tried not to be noticed, since every time she was noticed she garnered disapproval—not unusual in an alcoholic home.

Barbara's mother, a woman from a background of great privilege, was not the protector Barbara longed for and felt she deserved. Her mother never addressed her father's cruel jabs. Though often seductive around other men in the family's life, she fainted frequently as her way of dealing with the alcoholic in their home. Because there simply was no adult to soften blows or offer balance to Barbara's chaotic environment, Barbara tried to deal with her wounds on her own.

When, as an adult, she talked to her siblings about the past they had shared, she discovered that they hardly remembered her as a youngster. As children, they never banded together to minimize the trauma in the home—or, at least Barbara had not been included in "the band," if there was one. The pain about her chaotic past was heightened when, after looking through hundreds of pictures her grandfather gave the family, she noticed that she was only in two of them. Indeed, she had hidden herself from the activities that were occasions for photos. She had detached, as a child, but only physically. Emotionally, she absorbed every major slight and minor criticism.

▐▐▐▐▐

THE ENMESHMENT TRAP

Barbara's father had managed to get his law degree and to practice for a time, until one day, in his forties, he came home in the middle of the day and never went back to the office. His alcoholism was too advanced to expect anything different, and the family hardly noticed. The chaos in the home was much the same whether he was there or not.

One of the realizations Barbara has had in adulthood is that she and her father were very much enmeshed. He frequently told her he loved her and then emotionally beat her up. He often pitted Barbara against her older sister and seemed to enjoy the pain it caused. Barbara was often confused about how she should respond to him, but she loved him and desperately longed for those brief moments of attention and praise. She felt special when he separated from her mom for a time because of an affair and took her with him. When they returned home, Barbara felt rejected—a pattern that was to be felt and repeated many times in Barbara's life.

As Barbara grew older and began to separate herself from her parents, the verbal abuse from her father escalated. Her anxiety about pleasing other people escalated as well and followed her into her first marriage to Peter, an alcoholic. Her married life mirrored, in many ways, her life in her family of origin. She was always trying to do the right things so as not to incur the wrath of the drinker, and she was always fearful of rejection. She had never observed a healthy relationship, so she had no clue about how to create one.

When it became obvious that Peter's drinking wasn't normal, she followed the suggestion of a neighbor and went to Al-Anon for the first time. When she realized how highly developed her neediness and enmeshment were, she was really scared. Being enmeshed was like being mesmerized by a fire and unable to pull away, Barbara said. She was desperate for the help that Al-Anon offered. Fortunately, in Al-Anon she learned that she could remove herself from a situation that wasn't nurturing. She also became willing to call a friend when she was upset, particularly when her husband stayed away for days at a time.

Although Barbara desperately wanted to save their marriage, and Peter went to AA, in the end, the marriage didn't survive. When he ultimately remarried, Barbara was devastated at first and totally dependent on others for happiness. With the alcoholic out of her life, Barbara pulled away from Al-Anon meetings altogether. It wasn't that she didn't need the tools Al-Anon offered for her other relationships, but she didn't see how the tools could help her when the people in her other relationships were not alcoholic. She said she felt as though she lost all the knowledge she had gleaned from Al-Anon, almost overnight.

Barbara's romance with her second husband, David, began quickly. They moved in together in the first month. Her attachment to him was obvious to her but not suffocating to him. He didn't seem to notice it, in fact. They had an active social life and appeared to be happy for a few years. Then she noticed that he seemed to be pulling away. When she asked him about it, he denied doing so. She clutched more tightly, and the distance grew.

Her codependence and her neediness escalated to the point that he withdrew even more. Before their separation, she desperately tried to detach, suspecting that her insecurity was driving him away. But by the time he left, he had quit communicating in every way. Barbara was terrified when David left and felt extremely unsure of herself, but she threw herself into activities. She didn't want David or any of their friends to see that she needed him. She embarked on a new spiritual pathway, which gave her some solace, but she remained focused on what he had done to her. All she could think about was how she was devastated and how she had been betrayed once again. She struggled on a moment-by-moment basis, trying to feel okay as a single person once again. Even though she was trying to see the relationship's end as "the next right thing" for her life, she could only feel hurt and unlovable. Her new spiritual pathway had taught her that an action such as David's was, in essence, his cry for healing and help, but she couldn't embrace this idea. She simply wanted him to return and say that he still loved her.

It was not by accident that Barbara became friends with a woman who was in a Twelve Step recovery program. As their friendship grew, Barbara shared more and more about her family of origin and her two failed marriages. Her friend suggested that perhaps it was time for Barbara to return to Al-Anon. She resisted it at first, but her friend was persistent, even suggesting that she would join Barbara at the meeting. When Barbara did return, she found that her second exposure to Al-Anon was even richer in possibility than her earlier one.

卌

NO LONGER A CARETAKER OR VICTIM

The first time Barbara left Al-Anon, she had not gone to meetings long enough to understand the importance of transferring what she learned to "all of her affairs." Because her second husband wasn't alcoholic, Barbara hadn't considered turning to Al-Anon for support when he left. But on her return, she came to understand how the program's tools were as applicable to any relationship as they were to a relationship with an alcoholic.

With the help of Al-Anon, Barbara discovered how she naturally gravitated to being a needy caretaker as she got older in hopes of avoiding the cruel criticism she had grown so accustomed to. According to her earlier thinking, if she lovingly took charge of other people's lives in order to make their lives easier, they would need her and want her to stick around. Unfortunately, as her marriages and other relationships proved, doing for others what they need to do for themselves was no insurance against rejection. On the contrary, Barbara's caretaking tactics had resulted in plenty of rejection.

Barbara needed to explore the ramifications of her dependence on approval from men. It was rooted in her childhood with her father, and she carried the dependence through her teenage years and into adulthood. This dependence had caused her great pain through out her life, but through Al-Anon, she has been able to grow beyond it.

Barbara's life has changed dramatically since her return to Al-Anon. First, she is through with being a victim. In our interview, she said she had almost relished that role for years because it had allowed her to refuse responsibility for every detail of her own life. Now she defines detachment as "not claiming to be a victim." She has learned that detachment with love means choosing to separate herself from the situations over which she has no control. She says it also means being free of the need to make an emotional response, or any response at all, to a troubling person or a situation. She is able, now, to sense herself moving into her adult observer role. She has become adept at objectifying the details of her life.

Second, after much hard work, many meetings, lots of prayer, and unending willingness, Barbara has finally reached a place of forgiveness with her father, Peter, and David. She is still working on forgiving her mother, but she trusts that someday she will be able to.

Barbara is in another relationship now, and it is far different from those of her past. She is comfortable with a new balance between dependence and independence. Her new partner isn't an alcoholic, and he doesn't resemble in character or behavior either of her ex-husbands. For the first time in her adult life, she doesn't fear rejection, because she has grown secure in her knowledge that her Higher Power will always be with her. The neediness that plagued her for years is actually gone. And she says that when thoughts that aren't loving come to her mind, thoughts that are troubling in any way, she has learned to quietly say to herself, "Don't go there."

Al-Anon helped Barbara see who she was, where she was going, and where she wants to continue to go. She is now intent on sharing with others the tools that have transformed her life and dedication to carrying the message she has heard to many others. She has even volunteered to sponsor a weekly Alateen group, realizing that had she had access to one in her youth, she might have been spared years of pain and confusion. But she also believes that if she needed the past pain to get where she is now, she is grateful for it.

INSIGHTS

Barbara's transformation is available to any one of us who comes through the doors of a Twelve Step program. The timetable might be different, but the result is absolute if our willingness is genuine. And the real gift is that we can be transformed in *all* of our relationships. We don't have to be partnered with alcoholics or addicts to benefit from Al-Anon. We can utilize the principles offered in this simple, yet very wise program, in every situation, within every encounter we have, on a daily basis.

We generally come into Al-Anon, as Barbara did, for help in living with an alcoholic. But staying in Al-Anon promises us help in every relationship we'll ever have. What could be better than that?

6

RELIEF

KATY'S STORY

K ATY IS CLEAR THAT HER FEAR is what makes her want to control the actions of others. And she is clear about where the fear was first fostered. Not unlike most of the people I spoke to, Katy was the product of an alcoholic home. She was the youngest of three children and was sexually abused by her older brother when she was five years old. This trauma was never adequately acknowledged or addressed in an honest, loving way by her parents. Katy herself tried to get closure around the experiences but got no emotional support from her family.

Even though Katy's father got into recovery while she was still young, her mother never sought the help of Al-Anon or any type of counseling. The family never sought help for the challenges and heartache the alcoholism had caused, either. The problems were simply considered over and done with when Dad got sober.

Even though she proved to be an excellent student in high school, Katy felt inadequate. She had been motivated to excel at piano and ballet but the feelings of inferiority remained. So she often sought isolation, which she thought offered protection from the failure she was sure would happen when performing in the presence of others. While still in high school, Katy did rebel, for a time. She dumped the "nice boy" her parents approved of and fell madly in love with the "bad boy." Because she was threatening to run away with him, they sent her across the country to a strict girls' school, where her movements were monitored.

When she was in her first year of college, Katy met and married her first husband. They had two sons, but the marriage didn't last. She had finished college, so she was well employed, and the boys' father did his part to support them. Katy moved on with her life, but none of her imagined inadequacies were lessened in her first marriage or her time alone afterward. They were, in fact, heightened.

Her feeling of inadequacy was given even more of a boost in her second marriage. Her second husband initially appeared to be kind, sensitive, and loving toward her and her sons; however, his demeanor changed dramatically after they were married. During this marriage, Katy grew suicidal. Returning to school and changing careers briefly helped her self-confidence. However, she could see how controlled she was in the marriage, and she grew terrified of speaking her mind. Because of her husband's unyielding verbal abuse, she went along with his plans until she could no longer take the situation. For the sake of herself and her boys, she sought the guidance of a counselor and, with the counselor's support, decided to leave the marriage.

When I met Katy, she was in her third marriage. Because this husband, James, was in recovery for alcoholism, she had been introduced to Al-Anon, but James strongly mistrusted this program. Because Katy was extremely codependent, practicing the principles she learned in Al-Anon made her feel disloyal to James. Her belief that she was not good enough—a belief that grew out of the abuse she suffered—was as strong as it had been when she was a child. We attended the same meeting on a regular basis, and I could observe her fear firsthand every week. She was terrified to address the many defects I sensed her husband had. She wanted this marriage to last, and she wanted her emptiness filled. Week after week she came to the meeting. And week after week, I noted how sad and silent she was.

Yet because she kept coming to meetings, Katy painstakingly acquired the wisdom of Al-Anon. She never let her husband's mistrust of her involvement in Al-Anon keep her away. She committed to staying the course and was willing to "go to any lengths" to get well, as is suggested in the *Alcoholics Anonymous Big Book*.

Today, the evidence of her commitment and growth can be seen in a number of ways, and she eagerly pointed them out to me when I interviewed her. First, she has finally discovered her own voice. She says that sometimes she still has fear when she expresses herself, but she does so anyway.

Second, she knows, even when she doesn't practice it so well, that she is fundamentally okay, not just a body relying on another person's input to validate her. Having a sense of herself that isn't dependent on how others see her is still new, but refreshing and freeing. Detachment allows her to embrace herself; it encourages excitement in her and convinces her she can go anywhere, alone or with James. Life is no longer simply one crisis after another. She is aware of her choices. Likewise, she is aware of how limited her choices seemed to be when she was attached to her previous partners. For years she felt imprisoned, first to husband number one and then to husband number two. She visualizes her old behavior of attachment as wearing handcuffs.

Recalling this image acts as an alarm to her anytime she finds herself slipping into her old ways of thinking and behaving.

What Katy had feared for so many years, that she was alone in the universe, no longer troubles her. She does not doubt the presence of her Higher Power, and she recognizes that only this Higher Power deserves her undying attachment. Her most significant relationship is no longer fear based, and Katy can hardly contain her excitement over this change. She says she never really expected to attain the feelings of peace and happiness she now has.

Even more important, she says, is that when another person criticizes her or makes an outright attack, she doesn't feel diminished, at least not for long. Criticism used to destroy her; it could send her to her bed for hours, even days. Now she is able to see how others' judgments are about them, not her. This one simple change in her outlook has changed everything in her daily experience.

‖‖‖‖

INSIGHTS

Katy told me that one of the greatest gifts she has received from Al-Anon is the freedom to check in with friends in the program rather than with her significant other when she is considering making a life change of some kind. We can't get everything we need from a single source. Many of us came into Al-Anon meeting rooms quite insane because that's what we had attempted to do our entire lives. When we can't get the support and affirmation we yearn for from that one relationship, we are devastated and certain of our unworthiness. Counting on only a single person was and is a classic symptom of codependency.

One of the tools that has been effective for Katy is consciously observing detachment at work in the lives of many of the other Al-Anon people. She is fortunate to have joined Al-Anon groups that have a lot of old-timers in them. She has chosen her sponsors wisely, and she has made it a practice to watch them relate to their partners and to ask a lot of questions. Choosing to observe this way demonstrates her willingness to change. It also demonstrates how continuing to go to meetings and listening to the wiser people there helps us to begin to intuitively understand principles that may baffle us.

Katy is still climbing the ladder to full emotional health. She sometimes stays a little longer on a particular rung, and that's good. She has learned that it's not the pace of the climb but the constant commitment to the climb that matters. Her experience echoes one of the ideas I have come to cherish: the idea that I will never be done. There will always be more for me to learn. This fellowship, this pathway, my journey will not come to a close until I take my last breath. This thought gives me a lot of time, I hope, to continue growing in my love of others and celebrating the closer attachment that will result with my Higher Power. That's what our journey—both mine and Katy's—is about.

As Katy can attest, detachment doesn't come without hard work and a daily commitment to the effort, but the payoff is rewarding. Feeling good about yourself and feeling free to live your life in whatever way is pleasing to you are two gifts that detachment promises. Katy's experiences and the changes she has made offer such good examples to the rest of us. If she could begin to see positive possibilities in the stream of experiences she lived through, anyone can.

STRENGTH DOES COME

MARTHA'S STORY

ALCOHOLISM WEARS MANY MASKS, and one of these masks is extreme codependency, where we suffocate those whom we have designated as significant to our life. Martha definitely lived this trait before her drinking ever got her into trouble. She was caught in the web of codependency long before she was trapped by her alcoholism.

Although she seldom drank in the first three years of her marriage, she became addicted to prescription drugs. Her addiction was fueled, in large part, by her need to cope with her abusive husband. After she and her husband, Frank, bought a bar, Martha began drinking quite often, although she had some specific rules about where and when she would drink. One of the rules was that she would not drink when she was pregnant. But after each child was born, she'd return to drinking.

She noted that after each period of sobriety, she craved alcohol even more often. Soon she was also drinking in the mornings, and for the next few years, after her children were born, she drank heavily, morning, noon, and night. Even though she realized that alcohol had become a problem for her, she didn't want to quit. Drinking was her escape from a bad marriage that was characterized by a lot of verbal and emotional abuse. She didn't want to abuse her young kids while she was drinking, so she'd put them to bed very early every evening, so they would be "safe" when she began to drink.

Her husband was alcoholic, too, and Martha hated the way they were living their lives. Eventually the pain was great enough that she sought counseling, and her counselor promptly told her to go to AA. That suggestion triggered a memory for Martha. When she had been teaching school years previously, she had heard a couple of men tell their recovery stories. She recalled that the men were in AA and had been invited to a PTA meeting to discuss alcoholism. She also remembered that, even then, she suspected that she, too, was alcoholic, because they were describing the way she drank.

But she resisted going to AA. She knew she didn't drink as much as many of their friends and certainly not as much as her husband. One of the few times Frank supported her was in her resistance. "What would people think if my wife went to AA?" he asked. She didn't want to quit drinking, and she also didn't want to upset him, because the consequences would be too painful. So she didn't go.

[decorative gate symbol]

ESCALATING MISERY AND ANXIETY

Martha's drinking was certainly out of control, but it wasn't causing her as much pain as her relationship with her husband. She was dominated by him and constantly controlled by his dramatic mood changes. She could also feel herself growing dependent on the reactions of the people in her life. If they responded in a friendly way, she felt safe and at ease. If they were aloof or uncomplimentary, she was sure she had done something wrong. She recognized that she had transferred her way of reacting to Frank to all of the people around her. She didn't understand why; she knew only that her misery and her anxiety were escalating.

Out of desperation, she finally went to an AA meeting but told no one. She was a wreck emotionally, and she began going to meetings almost daily.

For the first few months in AA, she didn't feel the comfort and acceptance she sought. Again, she found herself basing her feelings on how others—this time the people in the meetings—were responding to her. As a result, she often left meetings feeling rejected and very much alone. Except for the fact that she wasn't getting drunk every night, nothing in her life seemed to be changing. She certainly wasn't feeling better emotionally. She might even have been feeling worse.

What Martha didn't understand was that her illness was two-pronged: she suffered from both alcoholism and codependency. Even though the alcohol had been removed from her life, her attachment to the whims and judgments of others had not lessened at all. In fact, that attachment was much more obvious to her now that she was sober.

She went back to her counselor, who suggested she try rational emotive therapy (now known as rational emotive behavioral therapy) to get control of her feelings. Martha had always been a good student, so this therapy technique seemed like a great solution. She could see how her feelings were the product of her own thoughts, and she could understand how changing her thoughts could produce different feelings. She began to feel more hopeful than she had felt in years.

Then her son, Jerry, began to abuse alcohol and drugs. This behavior quickly escalated into him physically abusing Martha and her daughter. Martha grew afraid of him, and she felt intense guilt, too. Had her disease caused his disease? He was certainly full of rage about her frequent absences from home for meetings when he was younger. Her sponsor and her counselor were preaching detachment, but Martha couldn't fathom what the word meant. Her son was very sick, and she saw it as her job, as a mother, to minister to him. More AA meetings seemed to be the answer, but little changed, for him or for Martha. She felt afraid for his safety and guilty for whatever part she had played in his illness.

Her husband compounded her problem by acting as though Jerry's problem were her fault. Eventually, he asked her for a divorce. She was devastated by the rejection and felt ashamed.

A REGULAR AT AL-ANON

After her divorce, Martha began to contemplate suicide. Fortunately, she ran into a friend who reminded her of the power of thoughts over feelings. This friend was also a regular at Al-Anon, and Martha decided to join her at a meeting.

Al-Anon gave Martha a new perspective. She left her hometown to start over in a new community, with new people, new meetings, new experiences. She sought a new career, going back to school—and excelling—at age fifty-five. After graduation she went to work in a new field and met Ralph, who became her second husband. They shared the recovery road. He was grateful to have a new wife who understood him, and she was grateful to have a loving husband who appreciated how she was living her life. Her relationships with her children had been strained since she left their hometown, but she prayed that in time they would be able to understand that the move had been necessary. She also applied the principles of Al-Anon every time her feelings became troubled.

All was well on the home front for a few years, until Ralph began to pull away. Martha noticed his withdrawal right away, but pretended she was imagining it. It wasn't fair to her that she should lose a marriage that had given her so much comfort. And she didn't understand why he wanted to leave. Hadn't she and Ralph had a wonderful way of communicating? Weren't they living their shared vision? He gave her no real explanation. He just wanted out. As he was struggling to be released, she began to hang on tight to him. What could she do if, at age sixty-three, she were cast aside? Dread and terror began to set in, and Martha could sense that she was reverting to her former self.

Her friends and sponsors were preaching once again, "Detach, detach, detach!"

Using the old tools of Al-Anon, Martha kept praying to feel grateful for her powerlessness. She said the Serenity Prayer over and over. And she listened to her sponsor and her friends remind her that God never takes away something or someone who should remain with you.

She tried to embrace the idea that if her second marriage were over, it would be because another door needed to open. She didn't really believe it at first, because Ralph's rejection felt so much more personal than her son's drug-induced behavior or her first husband's meanness. But she didn't give up her prayer for acceptance. She held her head up and kept going to meetings. She kept seeking guidance from her Higher Power and her sponsor. And she continued turning to the *Big Book* and her other program readings.

Little by little, she felt the fear and confusion lifting. A new job came Martha's way, giving her a new focus and helping her realize, once again, that she had so much to give. Even though the man she had hoped would value her for the rest of her life had failed to fulfill that dream, she was still needed. She still had many gifts to share with others, and God would always direct her to the best place for sharing them.

INSIGHTS

Even though Martha was the victim of a dual disease that knows no bounds, she lived through the pain and created a new life for herself. Today, she lives the principles of AA and Al-Anon. She never sought pity, only understanding and freedom from the bonds of others' reactions to her.

Martha is a survivor because she has learned that any kind of change is the result of changing our minds about how we see or experience a situation. One spiritual pathway says changing one's mind can be called a miracle. Indeed, there is great power in realizing and then utilizing this truth. We cannot change another person's mind, but we can and often must change our own. Adjusting our own attitudes is well within our power. How our lives are affected by others is the result of a simple decision: we can choose whether or not to be happy regardless of what another person is doing. Happiness is a by-product of the way we live our own lives, not the way others live theirs. No situation, no difficult person, no troublesome future event can trigger self-defeating behavior if we remember that no one and nothing has the power to take over our mind, thus our life.

Martha also learned how nothing will look quite the same if, in the midst of trying to control outcomes that are clearly not our business to control, we decide to let go and let God handle the turmoil. Even though her heart was aching to be attached to someone special, she strove to trust God and practice the principle of detachment. As a result, she has developed a sustaining relationship with her Higher Power that is wonderful to observe, particularly since she has been faced with some very painful relationships throughout her sobriety.

8

CHOOSING SURVIVAL

DANA'S STORY

THE ADDICTIONS THAT PLAGUED DANA were complicated. Alcohol, street drugs, and prescription drugs were the most evident addictions, but those people who knew her well realized she was just as dependent on certain people as she was on these substances. She seemed indifferent to the chaos in her life and rather mindlessly attached herself to anyone and anything that was offered to her. Once the attachment had occurred, she held on tight. It took many years and a lot of intervention to get Dana to release her hold on the many people and substances that had seemed to steady her when the chaos was reigning.

When Dana first "enrolled" in a recovery process, she clearly knew that she wanted some help. She just wasn't certain that she wanted to be rid of all of her addictions at one time. Going cold turkey after thirty-five years seemed impossible. When she was five years old, her dad began taking her to a bar, where she danced for the many men who were his cronies. They paid her with smiles, dimes, applause, kisses, and sips of their drinks. She loved the attention. She loved men. She loved having secret outings that her mom didn't know about. Her father seemed to like having her as an accomplice to his escapades. Keeping Dana's mom in the dark became a game they played frequently.

Dana's own use of alcohol started when she was twelve. Her dad kept a bottle of whiskey under the seat of his car, and Dana often helped herself. He never knew the difference, and even if he had, she doubted that he would have objected.

When Dana was sixteen she landed in the hospital with mononucleosis and severe colitis. She was in the hospital for three months and given numerous medications. It was the beginning of her thirty-five-year addiction to prescription drugs. Neither she nor her family saw the drugs as a problem. After all, the medications had been prescribed by a physician. Because the doctor had not suggested that using alcohol on top of the drugs was dangerous, Dana certainly saw no reason not to drink. She was doubly addicted in short order.

‖⊞⊞⊞‖

THE DIE WAS CAST

Six years, one marriage, and four children later, Dana was in serious trouble. Her husband was no help because he also had multiple addictions. Their marriage ended when Dana's youngest child was five, but Dana didn't care. She had formed liaisons with a number of men, and as long as she had someone to drink and drug with, she was content.

Dana's children never knew who was going to be there when they came home from school: a loving mother, a drug-enraged one, or none at all. Dana was sometimes absent from the home for two or three days at a time. She never told anyone she was leaving; she may well have not known, in all honesty. She simply followed the drugs and the man, whoever he might be. She was a hostage to them both.

Dana often lost track of where she was. Just as often, she didn't know some of the people she was with. Her lack of concern about her safety was due more to being under the influence of mood-altering chemicals than to having courage. She was accustomed to being attached to a male figure, and as long as one was around, she felt safe. When she was a child, her dad had made her feel special and protected, and as an adult, she felt herself protected by whomever she was with.

Even in her adulthood, Dana and her father remained protective of each other's addictions. He covered for her when she disappeared from home. She took his side when he was caught in an argument with her mother. They were bonded in an unhealthy way. But when he went to treatment and tried to change his life, Dana felt betrayed and feared the loss of his protection. However, he didn't give up his prescription drugs, only his alcohol consumption. He was still as easily manipulated as before. Their bond held, and their conspiracy continued.

While still in the throes of addiction to street drugs and alcohol, Dana suffered from chronic colitis and was diagnosed with lupus. The lupus caused a great deal of pain in her joints. Being able to justify prescription painkillers gave Dana an excuse to stay addicted, and she had the family physician to write the prescriptions. People were afraid of her drug-induced rages, so no one confronted her. She loved this power she had over people.

Dana's dependence on men and drugs took their toll on her kids. The patterns they observed and began to imitate foreshadowed many problems. Dana's oldest daughter became a drug addict and a runaway while in her early teens. Her son was full of rage and frequently in trouble with the law. Dana's second daughter also suffered with chronic colitis and used addictive painkillers. Her youngest daughter had an eating disorder and frequent panic attacks. None of them ever felt at peace. All were hostages to substances and circumstances outside themselves.

Dana's family was spinning out of control, but she expressed neither concern nor interest in seeking a solution to the insanity. This insanity had, in fact, become normal. As long as it didn't keep her from her drugs, she could ignore it.

TREATMENT OR JAIL

Fortunately, other people who lived on the fringes of the family could not ignore the insanity. A friend finally called the authorities about the drug use in the home. Dana was given a choice: go to treatment or jail. She didn't really prefer treatment; in fact, she thought jail might be a lark. One of her lovers was a paroled convict, and his past had seemed pretty exciting to her. But longtime family friends convinced her to give treatment a try, and her kids pleaded that treatment would give their family a chance to stay together. So she reluctantly went to treatment, resisting every step of the way.

Dana was part of a woman's treatment unit and didn't like it one bit. There were no men to seduce, no one to manipulate, no one to prance in front of. Ellen, her counselor, had been much like Dana before Ellen got sober; she was able to look Dana in the eye and read her mind. Once Dana decided to give up her game, her growth began.

One of the first things Dana learned from her treatment peers was that she could feel okay whether she had a man in her life or not.

She didn't believe it. She had never relied on herself to feel okay. She had always hung on to the words of men who only wanted a sexual, drinking partner. They told her what she wanted to hear, and she did what they wanted to do.

Ellen also convinced Dana to put her kids first—something Dana didn't actually know how to do. Her children had never come first in her life. In fact, for most of her mothering years, she had seldom thought of them at all. Because the drugs and men took precedence, she seldom noticed parenting obligations. When Dana left treatment, she found that mothering, in and of itself, was overwhelming. Just getting meals and making sure there were clean clothes for everyone to wear to school wore Dana out the first week home. Because she had not paid attention to her family's needs for a long time, she hadn't realized how attentive her parents had been to her kids for the past few years. Her shame was great, and her guilt made her angry and resentful. She didn't understand her feelings, but Ellen had advised her to talk them over with other women who were in recovery. She tried it and learned that her new friends in her post-treatment support groups and other women in recovery didn't judge her. And she went to meetings, got a sponsor, and put men on the back burner. She also began to learn that when someone disagreed with her, she could handle it without drinking, crying, or running to a man. The freedom she began to feel surprised her, and she had hope for the first time in years. She actually had not even realized how "out of hope" she had been for most of her adult life.

|++++++|

A NEW JOB: BEING MATURE

Dana went to Al-Anon along with AA, as had been suggested in her treatment. (Her first sponsor attended both groups, too.) Al-Anon told her that her job was not to make others happy, but to be a mature, responsible parent.

She has now been clean and sober for more than twenty years. She has learned how to have male friends, and she has opted to remain single, choosing instead to be the kind of grandmother she never imagined she would willingly be. The many things she had not done as a mother she is now eager to do as a grandmother. Playing games, having long talks, reading books, and traveling with her grandkids take the place of drugs and men. She has the unconditional love of her six grandchildren and the respect of four children. She is still prone to be a bit too attached to certain people, but at least the people she gets attached to do not use or abuse her.

Dana wakes up every day knowing where she is and how she wants to spend the day. Even better, she wakes up knowing she is responsible for only herself. She no longer suffers because of someone else's actions or reactions. Never again will she let herself be abused or used by someone else for any reason.

▐▬▬▬▬▬▐

INSIGHTS

When she left treatment, Dana's sponsor, Ellen, gave her a few words of advice: "Learn to detach from the unhealthy attention of others." Dana had no idea what that really meant, but Ellen insisted she talk it over with the other women in her program. "You can learn," Ellen said.

Ellen, AA, and Al-Anon told Dana she would grow in healthy ways if she kept showing up and listening to the old-timers. She was told that spiritual progress was possible, and it would allow her to see her potential as a woman and a mother. She was told, again and again, that her fears would go away. It was especially hard for her to believe the last promise, because her fears had haunted her for years. But her new friends assured her that they had come into recovery just as scared and resistant to these new ideas as she was, and she could see that they were now happy. For the first time in her life, Dana began to listen to the guidance of people who were not using chemicals of any kind.

If the disease one is living with is codependency, there is no more comforting a place to be exposed to healthier behaviors than an Al-Anon meeting. Dana's story shows how as long as we continue to go to meetings and listen to the wiser ones there and read our literature, we will begin to know intuitively what may baffle us at first. As a friend of mine says, if we just keep showing up at meetings, the program will "get us." We change more easily when we are in the company of others who are changing too. We see more clearly when we are in the presence of others who have greater clarity. What we see and hear is imprinted on our minds. The principles we learn by going to meetings, listening to sponsors, working the Twelve Steps, and vigilantly seeking to know our Higher Power give each of us hope, as they did for Dana. If we don't absorb our lesson when it is first offered, we will have other opportunities to learn it if we keep listening to others. Like Dana, we will learn what we need to learn. Then we will become the teachers for others who are in our lives.

Becoming a teacher is exactly what Dana has done. She has become a counselor, working with others who are so much like her old self. She became willing to learn how "to walk the walk," and now she is a role model, particularly for women who found themselves addicted to the men in their lives. Other women can relate to her story and realize that they, too, can break the addictive cycles in their lives.

Dana well represents the idea that we strengthen in ourselves that which we are intent on sharing with others. We will only be able to maintain our peacefulness if we give away and share what we have learned. The wisdom that we can share with others makes the circle complete. We must give away the wisdom we have received or we will not be able to keep it!

9

A SPIRITUAL ACTION

RAYMOND'S STORY

RAYMOND SAYS HE NEVER IMAGINED his life would change from what it was. He had assumed he would always drink until he was drunk, day in and day out.

Raymond grew up in the Midwest. His father seldom drank, but the first time Raymond got drunk was at age eleven, on some home brew his dad had made. By the time Raymond was fourteen, he was getting drunk regularly. His mother had started drinking, too, and she quickly became an alcoholic right along with her son. Raymond's father was beside himself with grief over what was happening to both of them. Raymond kept promising himself and his dad that he would stop, but he didn't keep those promises.

He married a woman who came from an alcoholic family, and so he didn't have to explain his drinking patterns. For the first few years of their marriage, Mary accompanied Raymond to the bars, drinking along with him, as she had watched her mother do for so many years.

After the children were born, Raymond went to the bars alone, which was fine with him. His cronies were always there and generally without their spouses, too. Most of his friends, fellow postal workers, were also alcoholic. Since they all "wore the badge," they protected one another whenever one of them was too drunk to make it home or deliver the mail the next day. He felt lucky to have this special group of people watching out for him.

However, Mary was getting tired of his drinking, and after one serious drunken automobile accident, she threatened to take the children and leave. He didn't believe her and resumed his former pattern of drinking soon after returning to work. She, in turn, didn't follow through with her threat.

In his thirties, Raymond realized that booze had become a problem. He was having blackouts, and he knew they were not normal. He could generally remember where his drinking had begun, but he recalled little after that. Mary again threatened to leave, and this time she actually did, taking their kids to California. For an entire month, she was gone, and throughout the month, Raymond refrained from drinking—the longest period he had been sober since age fourteen.

Unfortunately, his sobriety didn't last. Soon after Mary's return from California, Raymond resumed drinking. He was thrilled that she had returned. He wanted her and the kids in his life. He just couldn't commit to leaving the alcohol out of his life. His disease had progressed significantly by then, and he missed work frequently, relying on "the boys" to cover for him.

Almost before Raymond realized it, he and Mary were celebrating their twenty-fifth wedding anniversary. She had started going to

Al-Anon, and Raymond had agreed to go to AA. But his resolution
to not drink was intermittent. He spent three years attempting to "stay
with the solution," but the draw to drink was strong. Finally, in exas-
peration, Mary sued for divorce. As is typical of the scared alcoholic,
Raymond vowed never to drink again, and for one month, he didn't.
Mary dropped her proceedings.

▉▉▉

SOBRIETY AT LAST

At first, Raymond was not totally abstinent, but his drinking
decreased. Surprisingly, he discovered that he liked AA and the
people he met there. Even more surprisingly, he began to suspect
they liked him, too. He had never felt this comfortable except with
the postal workers he had been working and drinking with.

Raymond began doing the work of AA newcomers with relish.
He made the coffee, set up the chairs, gave people rides. He liked
belonging. And he liked that no one told him to stay away when he
had been drinking. He was accepted for who he was, and he always
had a place to be now that he was trying to stay out of the bars.

His last experience of being drunk was on his annual fishing trip with
the guys. He had promised his wife he wouldn't drink, but his resolve was
soon spent. He got sick all over the motel room and was mortified. He
knew the woman who owned the motel, and he hated to have to face her
and Mary. After that experience, he never drank again.

Today, Raymond loves to tell stories about his grandchildren and
his children. He missed so much of the upbringing of his own kids
because he was away drinking or too drunk while at home to be present in the events in their lives, and he is compensating for those losses
by showing up for his grandkids. He rejoices at the realization that he

can play cards and go to parties and have people over without needing to consider alcohol.

Raymond is a man filled with gratitude for a fellowship that always includes laughter, wonderful suggestions from others for how to live more peacefully, and the constant contact with "the God of his understanding" that is a by-product of being in a Twelve Step program. He is grateful for his family, for his reconnection to his religious roots, and for his good health. He relishes the possibilities he sees for living the rest of his life in this peaceful realm and having the principles of AA to sustain him. He had not expected sobriety to be rewarding, fun filled, or interesting.

|++||++|

INSIGHTS

Unlike most of the people I interviewed for this book, Raymond has never been controlled by the actions of others, which is one of the reasons his story is so intriguing to me. I had spent most of my life, certainly all of my life prior to recovery, trying to live others' lives for them or at least trying to make them live their lives according to my plans. I hadn't even tried to quit controlling others until I'd been in Al-Anon for months. That Raymond has never needed to do that absolutely stuns me.

He seems to have the natural gift for detaching from and not reacting to the whims of others. When he was drinking, his wife's anger never really got to him, nor did the threat of the "big bosses" at work. He was able to roll with the punches. When his wife threatened to leave or served him with divorce papers, he wasn't happy, but he wasn't immobilized. And he didn't strike back. He had spent his life exactly as he wanted to spend it, following his own inclinations rather than those of others, regardless of the consequences.

Then, when starting down the recovery road, he didn't come into the fellowship of AA assuming that he would find what others may have found. Not knowing what to expect, his attitude was one of "wait and see." He now seems to treat newcomers with the same "wait and see" philosophy, welcoming everyone and taking people as they are. Because his own journey took a number of detours, he is able to let others journey wherever they need to go before they settle in. And he is always there with open arms when the wayward return. His natural ability to let others be whoever they are and not pass judgment on them is serving him well in his recovery and in his efforts to help others in theirs. He is particularly disappointed that one of his daughters is alcoholic and not yet interested in recovery. But he loves and accepts her and does not preach to her. He knows she knows how to reach out to him if she wants his help.

Raymond embodies the slogan, "Live and let live" by his every word and deed. He is always supportive of those who struggle. His actions in any situation are thoughtful and nonjudgmental. He practices detachment with no effort, without even realizing or taking credit for it. And because of his highly developed sense of healthy detachment, he possesses an enviable peacefulness and serenity. I am convinced that this would be a better world if all of us interacted with one another in the way that Raymond so naturally does.

SLOGANS AS MEASURING STICKS

In many AA and Al-Anon meeting rooms, slogans are taped to the walls, along with the Twelve Steps and the Twelve Traditions. I can well remember my reaction to the slogans when I first came into recovery: I nearly gagged on them as "principles" for living. I was a graduate student, for heaven's sake! My philosophy for living was far more erudite than these simple phrases.

I am ashamed to admit it but, initially, my college-educated judgment hindered me from seeing the slogans of Al-Anon and AA as valuable life principles. Fortunately, there are enough old-timers around who want to keep growing by continuing to give the wisdom they gained to skeptics like me. When I became willing to listen to what others were saying in the meetings, I heard the slogans often. My sponsor and individuals I respected at meetings used them as touchstones for their well-being on a day-to-day basis.

I now see the slogans as shortcuts to the attainment of detachment. "Keep it simple," "let go and let God," and "live and let live" can serve as shorthand for understanding the concept of detachment and for doing an immediate check of our own behavior in a particular instance. Measuring ourselves against a slogan at a moment's notice will show us where we stand.

Let me explain by turning to "keep it simple." That was the slogan I immediately noticed on the wall as I entered my first meeting room. I couldn't fathom what it meant. My life felt complicated, and I liked it that way. From my troubled perspective, it meant I was intriguing and rich in experiences. It also meant that I had intertwined my life around the lives of everyone on my path. I was attached to myriad people, places, and things. I was defined by my attachments, and I thought that was good. I can remember feeling sorry for people who didn't have a complicated assortment of people they fretted over all the time. I attributed their detachment to boredom, disinterest, or avoidance of others. Whatever the case, it wasn't something to be proud of.

The idea of keeping your life simple by staying out of situations that don't directly involve you, thus freeing you to live only your own life, had not occurred to me. My life was about other people, and I was always in turmoil. Yet the old-timers in Al-Anon who practiced keeping their lives simple were peaceful. They expressed joy. Their foreheads were not perpetually furrowed, as mine was. Their outlook and demeanor eventually became attractive to me.

Keeping it simple is one of the main antidotes to turmoil and anxiety, which are in turn, two causes of the relapse to alcohol or drugs that many experience. I was able to appreciate the value of keeping it simple only when I spent time with those who kept it simple. I wanted what they had. Actual, healthy detachment was still a long way off, but I was finally able to see that living with detachment was far superior to the way I had been living.

Using the slogans whenever and wherever possible will help us immensely to keep from taking a hostage or being a hostage to someone else. Keeping it simple, living one day a time, and letting go and letting God do the work that is God's changes every single aspect of our lives. Releasing our attachment to others comes naturally when we are making use of the slogans on a regular basis.

FOLLOWING THE FOOTSTEPS

CLAIRE'S STORY

CLAIRE IS AN ATTRACTIVE WOMAN who laughs easily. Her wit is sharp, and she seems able to assess situations quickly. One of the things I liked immediately is her willingness to ask questions when she is confused. She is not afraid to let others know that she doesn't understand something. It's a refreshing trait and suggests that she is comfortable with who she is.

Claire was the oldest with four siblings. She said her addiction to chemicals initially surprised her, since she had not been parented by addicts. Shaking the family tree produced a few alcoholics, though. In Claire's immediate family, depression was the disease that contributed to dysfunction. Her mother spent many months of many years in bed with depression. Interestingly enough, her grandmother spent many complete years in bed: she fell ill at age sixty and didn't get out of bed for the next thirty-six years. Claire said she didn't find these circumstances unusual at the time. They were accepted by everyone as normal and were not even discussed. In retrospect, she sees the dysfunction clearly.

Claire went through her teens without a drink or a cigarette. But when she got to college, all hell broke loose. Dexedrine became her drug of choice. The family physician prescribed it because he thought she was chubby. She wasn't, she now sees, but her addictions were set in motion. For more than twenty years, she succumbed to the addiction of one thing after another, including other people. Even though amphetamines remained her drug of choice, like many of us, she was willing to take anything offered to her. Pills accompanied her into two marriages. She had no inkling that her using behavior was abnormal. Most of her friends were on Dexedrine, too. Doctors indiscriminately dispensed the pills to patients who wanted to be thin or have more energy, because the medical community at the time was unaware of the dangers of Dexedrine.

Claire was pretty much disconnected from her family during these two marriages, but she didn't see that as strange. That the love in her family seemed conditional didn't matter to Claire. Her family members weren't really on her radar screen. They led their lives; she led hers. What did surprise her, however, was how much her own life was beginning to mimic her mother's. In one eight-year period, Claire was hospitalized eight times for depression. She actually liked those times, because they gave her relief from trying to do the work of a wife and mother—work at which she felt unsuccessful.

Her second husband was a great caregiver. He had learned this behavior well, having grown up with a mentally ill mother who looked to him for care. Claire's behavior grew reckless when she drank under the influence of pills. Her infidelity troubled her but not enough for her to stop it or her drinking.

After her divorce, she went to a therapist, who suggested she go to AA. In addition to alcohol, she willingly gave up Dexedrine. But instead of weaning herself from the pills gradually, as her doctor had suggested, she went cold turkey. Claire didn't know that withdrawal from addictive drugs needs to be closely monitored, and she only narrowly avoided a medical condition that might have been fatal.

▮▮▮▮▮▮

NOTICING THE WORLD

Claire wasn't comfortable with AA at first, and after a few meetings, she contemplated suicide. Fortunately, she went to treatment before her situation worsened. In the aftercare portion of the treatment, a counselor significantly changed her life by asking a simple question: "Do you ever see the sunrise or the sunset? That's just for you, you know."

What he meant was that she should notice these natural phenomena, notice the world around her. She began to do just that. Her son "came into view," as did her friends, her house, and her yard with all its flowers. Suicide still intrigued her, but she kept following the assignments she was given by her sponsors and other friends in AA. One of the assignments was to go to Al-Anon, which helped her develop boundaries in her relationships with others.

One aspect of Claire's life remained unchanged even after committing herself to Al-Anon: she continued to struggle with depression. Being a double winner—someone who benefited from both AA and Al-Anon—had always made her feel lucky, but she seldom felt real joy or hope for the future. She was relieved to have places to go to talk about her continuing struggles with the relationships in her life, but she wasn't getting free of the emotional baggage of those relationships.

AA and Al-Anon meetings had definitely provided safety valves for her, but they did not lift the depression that haunted her.

Because of the severity of her depression, she finally sought the help of a psychiatrist, who prescribed an antidepressant. Like many in AA, she resisted antidepressants initially, but after hearing the stories of others whose lives had improved after finally taking them, she agreed to try them.

The change wasn't immediate, but when it came, it was profound. The element that seemed to change most was her ability to let others be whoever they needed to be. What surprises her the most, she says, is that she can now love people even when they don't do as she wishes. That's detachment—unadulterated detachment.

Her parting words to me were "I live in a state of peace now. As soon as something begins to engage my ego, I pray and the something fades." It's possible and even probable that every one of us can do what Claire is able to do if that's what we desire, if that's what we ask our Higher Power for, and if we are willing to ask again and again, every time we try to take back the control.

▦▦▦

INSIGHTS

Hard as she tried, for a long time Claire still found the actions of others often put her into a tailspin. Intellectually understanding her powerlessness over others was not beyond her reach, but feeling emotionally good about their distance was difficult. She wanted others to think of her first. She wanted them to lead their lives her way.

Today Claire is actually grateful that the lives of others are none of her business. This knowledge makes her free—free to be happy, free to walk away from situations that are not helpful to her and from people who are not kind to her, free to watch others do whatever they choose to do. Remembering that we are not in charge is not so bad once we get used to it. In fact, like Claire, most people come to relish the idea. Learning to get over whatever is not going our way is the easiest and fastest change we can make in our lives—and one of the most fruitful.

Claire, for example, has found that her freedom gives her so much extra time to do the fun activities she thought she never had time to do. She now realizes that getting too involved in the lives of others only complicates the picture of our lives; being responsible for ourselves and no one else means we have more time than we'd ever imagined to pursue fascinating lives. We can follow our heart's desire rather than someone else's without feeling guilty. Like Claire, we can both accept and celebrate that we did have only our own lives to be fully responsible for.

However, lest we forget, Al-Anon also helps us realize that we are not entirely in charge of even our own lives. Our Higher Power is directly involved. And Claire reminds us that the Third Step, making the decision to turn her life over to her Higher Power, has taught her that her life is not her business, but God's business. But as long as her security and happiness were tied to what others are doing, she couldn't see her Higher Power's role in her own life.

Like Claire, we are not able to hear the messages God is trying to send us about our lives if we are focused on being in charge of another's actions or feelings. Every one of us is here to do God's work, but we cannot hear our call to do that work if we are cajoling and nagging the others who surround us. As long as we stay tied to another person, we will not be free to travel the path that is divinely our own. When we turn our lives over to our Higher Power, as Claire has learned to do, events may not turn out as we'd intended, but they will be more in keeping with God's plan for us, and we will end up being where we need to be when it's our time to be there.

II

TEMPERING THE INNER FIRE

MORRIE'S STORY

MORRIE, LIKE CLAIRE, came into recovery through AA. A daily drinker, he got his "education" at the feet of his hard-drinking Scottish parents, though at the time, he didn't know they were alcoholic. Morrie's mom suffered not only with alcoholism but also with depression. She frequently spent many days in bed, offering no explanation to her family as to why she did. Meanwhile, Morrie's dad was not very communicative, and Morrie and his brother were simply left on their own.

Morrie entered the military immediately after high school. Upon leaving the Military, he found work in the construction business. Fortunately for Morrie, who was a hot-tempered young man and tended to lose jobs, the demand for workers exceeded the supply. Salaries were high, and the atmosphere of plenty made the post-work stop at the saloon an everyday occurrence. Morrie figured he worked hard, so he deserved a few rounds with the guys. Unfortunately, he didn't always make it home, and when he did, it was simply to drop into bed for a few short hours before repeating the pattern all over again. Morrie's dad suggested that he lay off the booze, but Morrie could not hear it.

Morrie met his wife, Cora, at the neighborhood firehouse, one of his drinking haunts. He was enamored of her right away because of her beauty and her quietness. Though she was married when they first met, she divorced a short time later, and Morrie was delighted. Cora had left her first husband because he was an alcoholic and very abusive. She had no idea she was climbing from the frying pan into the fire. Morrie adopted Cora's daughter. He was happier than he had ever imagined he could be—until Cora began to nag him about his drinking and his late hours.

His relationship with Cora, their daughter, and then their son suffered a great deal because of his drinking. He really didn't notice, but Cora did and insisted he do something about it. After losing yet another job, he finally went to an AA meeting.

At first, Morrie just couldn't see how sitting around with a bunch of drunks, many of whom were not working, could help him or how they could have anything to say that he needed to hear. But he was surprised that no one in the meetings judged him or shamed him or sent him away. In fact, they were quick to say, "Welcome back." Even Jackie, the first person he ever spoke to at a meeting, didn't scold him. Morrie somehow knew from that moment on that he would never have to drink again, and he hasn't.

Morrie says he remembers being told by a young woman in a meeting that one day he would find a joy that was beyond his wildest imagination. Instead, he says, the joy found him. Now, every chance he gets, he tells others what he was told: someday, a joy beyond your wildest dreams will find you. Before AA, being calm was an unknown experience for Morrie. He had thrived in chaos. When chaos didn't happen as the result of others' actions, he created it. Now Morrie says that he still cannot believe he deserves the peace he feels. And his wife, Cora, says she can't believe Morrie is the same man she married.

〰️

INSIGHTS

Even though Morrie never has been a member of Al-Anon, he has managed to incorporate the most important of Al-Anon's principles into his everyday life: he detaches from those situations and events that don't personally concern him or affect his well-being. Morrie used to assume it was his business to control how everything was being done by everybody who worked or lived around him. Even after he retired from the world of union bosses and big construction projects, he made it his business to oversee the activities of his children, his wife, his brother, and his neighbors. But he experienced the transformation that comes from inviting our Higher Power into our minds every time we feel obsessed with another's behavior vying for a foothold.

For Morrie, the Serenity Prayer has become almost a mantra. As many times a day as necessary, he asks God for the wisdom to know what his business is, and he lets the rest go. He also reminds himself that his only assignment is to do the next right thing. Some of the activities of others still bother him, he admits, but he is willing to own his failed attempts to move his mind away from whatever situation claims his unwanted attention.

Now, on those occasions when he does become negatively engaged by the actions of others, he uses a simple tool: walking away. Sometimes he mutters under his breath while doing so, but he still walks away.

Again, at times like these, the Serenity Prayer brings him back to God and the peace he has grown to cherish. Though sometimes he is still quick to get angry, Morrie walks away from situations over which he has no control. When I spoke with him, he exclaimed, again and again, how amazed he is that it is possible to walk away from any chaos that surrounds him. After speaking with him, I have come to believe that every one of us can learn how to walk away, as Morrie does.

Another important thing Morrie has learned is to pray for those individuals who get under his skin. When Jackie first suggested this idea to him, he balked. He had handled so many situations with his fists in the past that to do nothing, followed by actually praying for the person, was at first beyond his comprehension. He refused to even try praying for the other person for quite some time, in fact. Then one day, when he was overwhelmed with rage at a neighbor, he tried it. He was amazed at how quickly his rage left him, and he was even more amazed at how calm he felt right on the heels of the prayer. He has not forgotten that solution, and he shares it with others often.

12

FELLOWSHIP THROUGH
THE BACK DOOR

JUDY'S STORY

J
UDY'S FAMILY OF ORIGIN WAS different from the families of
the many stories in this book. When she shook her family tree,
no alcoholics fell out. But because she was raised in a Catholic home
and attended a Catholic grade school, she accumulated her share of
shame. Her second-grade teacher, for example, scolded her for not
being more like Jesus. Her failure to live up to this standard instilled
a sense of perpetual shame that occasionally still trips her up. To this
day, she occasionally lacks confidence in some of the situations she
must address personally and professionally.

Fortunately, the teacher's denouncement was not validated in her experiences at home, so Judy did not become as insecure as she might have. She says her upbringing was not typical; at least it was not similar to what her friends have told her about their upbringing. On one hand, her parents never really knew how she felt about anything because they never asked her, and the words "I love you" were seldom spoken. On the other hand, she didn't feel unloved, and she had a lot of freedom as long as she followed the rules.

Judy's mother died when Judy was in her early twenties. Even though Judy doesn't feel they had a lot of unfinished business, she didn't get to ask many of the questions she realizes now she would like answered. The realization of missed opportunities has informed many of her actions, thoughts, and dreams since that time. She knows firsthand that time is fleeting. She does not want to leave unsaid or unasked those questions that might guide her or trouble her. She knows that anything she says to a friend, a colleague, a spouse, or other family member might be the last word she ever says to that person. She wants no regrets.

Judy's profession brought her into contact with the addicted as well as those in the recovering community. These relationships fostered her need and her desire to know more about the diseases of alcoholism and addiction. They also taught her the value of a having a Twelve Step program in one's life. She observed firsthand the clear guidance it offered other people, and realized she wanted what they had. She began going to Al-Anon, not for the same reasons that family members of alcoholics might, but because she could see how much more directed and even peaceful the lives of Al-Anon participants were. She was envious of their path. And since in her workplace she was surrounded by alcoholics in recovery and in the active addiction stage, she figured she had a need for Al-Anon, too. She understood that every person alive is affected by someone's alcoholism, if not directly, than certainly indirectly. Meeting the man who was to become her husband clinched her need for Al-Anon. He was a recovering addict who was committed to the Twelve Steps as a way of life.

|··||||||··|

KEEP WHAT FITS, LEAVE THE REST

Judy was a quick study and took to the Al-Anon program eagerly. She much appreciated the spiritual direction it offered, since she had not remained active in the church of her youth. She realized right away how the program principles could help her let the outcomes of others' behaviors be their problem, not hers.

At one of her first meetings, she heard that she could "keep what fits and leave the rest." She heard this message read at the end of every meeting, too. She wasn't entirely sure what this principle meant initially, but she observed how no one ever disagreed with anyone else's comments in a meeting. There were no arguments, and she heard no discussion about who was right or wrong after the meetings. This lack of disagreement astounded her, particularly because not every statement agreed with every other statement. Whatever was said was the opinion of the speaker. Eventually she understood that "keep what fits and leave the rest" ensured the free flow of discussion and sharing.

Judy quickly saw how going to Al-Anon meetings helped her in her professional life as well as her personal life. On a regular basis, she began to evaluate what the next right thing to do was. It became apparent that one of the next right things was to marry the recovering addict whom she had been dating. She was also certain that continuing to work in the field of addictions was what her life purpose was about. Both decisions were guided by the Al-Anon principles she had grown to cherish.

Judy's marriage is one area of her life that still causes angst. She loves her husband and is a "lifer" when it comes to marriage, but she has to steer a careful course between his needs and her own. She knows it's far too easy to pass by her own needs while trying to meet his. When she ignores her own needs in favor of his, she feels resentful, he can detect her resentment, and neither of them is truly happy.

Communication is their solution when a conflict arises. Although Judy didn't observe much conflict in her family, she doesn't recall seeing or experiencing much healthy communication either. When our family of origin doesn't offer examples of healthy behavior for us to imitate, we must find guidance elsewhere. Because of her association with the Twelve Steps, Judy has found many great communication role models. One of the gifts she has gained from her involvement with Al-Anon has been the courage to clearly tell her husband what she hopes a particular outcome will be. They may not end up agreeing on the best outcome, but they are able to compromise and then decide on a solution that is acceptable to both. The key element is that they are able to get to this solution peacefully because both are committed to the Twelve Steps for life.

|||||||||

INSIGHTS

Because Judy has been an active participant in the Al-Anon fellowship for years, she had many suggestions on how to find the peace and joy that she has found.

The first thing she offered was her definition of detachment: "It's doing the next right thing without focusing on the outcome." She says she has had to learn who she really is in order to evaluate what is coming toward her and feel confident that she is doing the next right thing. When she is troubled by anxiety, she copes by seeking solutions that are immediate, simple, and centered on her Higher Power. Detachment has become her spiritual approach to life.

One of the key "miracles" promised through Al-Anon, from Judy's perspective, is the ability to step back, assess what's going on, and realize that her life is not dependent on what others are doing. At one point in her life, she was consumed by her sensitivity to how everyone around her was responding to her and to each other. She has freed herself from this obsession through the work she has done in the Al-Anon fellowship. Most things that seem to be happening to her need not be taken personally.

Being free of the compulsion to take everything too personally leads to another profound lesson that Judy has learned. When we choose not to let what another person does or says determine how we feel, we free ourselves to choose our own response. When a clerk is rude, a spouse is discounting, a child is disrespectful, or a friend confronts us, we do not have to take the person's remarks or behavior personally and feel diminished as a human being. Instead, we can step back and say to ourselves, "What part of this experience can I learn from, and what part should I simply let go of?"

It is very helpful to ask ourselves if the situation warrants a response, forgiveness, prayer, or the decision to let go of the remark, realizing that most remarks that are not loving are coming from the other person's fearful ego. Every experience—no matter what kind of interaction it is between two people—is "managed" by either the ego or the Higher Power within. When the latter is in charge, our response to the situation will be loving, no matter how we feel. Judy's shorthand way of remembering this principle is to say to herself: "Stuff happens. How can I deal with it? What's the path of love through it? How might I help others see the path of love if that is their choice?"

Thanks to this perspective, Judy is now able to celebrate the fact that everyone has his or her own journey, and she does not need to give others her input unless it's asked for. Al-Anon has taught Judy that she is only a small part of the process for change in a person's life. She knows she can be an example of how another person might choose to live. She can also offer her experience, strength, and hope when it is requested. But she knows she must refrain from telling others what they have to do. That knowledge relieves her of the obsessive need to watch or attempt to control what another person is choosing to do next. Learning that she doesn't have to be anyone else's Higher Power has been one of the gifts she has received from Al-Anon. This lesson has been extremely useful in her professional work with clients, and it translates well into her personal life, too.

When explaining the concept of detachment to her sponsees, Judy tells them that they are not the "target, the subject, of all that other people may be thinking who are sharing their journey." In other words, we are not the center of everyone's universe, no matter how much we want to be. But being detached doesn't mean we are distant from everyone. Rather, it means we are in relationships in a loving, accepting, noncontrolling way. We are close to the significant people in our lives, but we are not stuck to those people.

Judy is a great, living example of the power of detachment. She is secure, inner directed, spiritual, open to the thoughts of others, and not defensive or argumentative. She expresses empowerment in a humble way because she does not depend on her colleagues or her friends to live life her way, on her terms, or according to her timetable.

13

FROM DARKNESS TO DAWN

KATHLEEN'S STORY

KATHLEEN IS THE YOUNGEST CHILD in her family, having two older sisters and an older brother. Both parents were alcoholic and drug dependent, and their obsession with scoring drugs and using alcohol made them unavailable parents much of the time. When Kathleen was five years old, her dad unexpectedly divorced her mother and moved to another city. In response, her mother retreated even more into her alcohol and drugs, leaving the four children to try to fend for themselves. Although she was devastated by her father's departure, Kathleen tried her best to make her mother happy so Mom wouldn't hide in her bedroom and drink, but this task was impossible for a little girl.

Kathleen's oldest sister stepped in to play mother, but she, too, began to use drugs at an early age. By the time Kathleen was in school full time, she didn't know whom she could count on to be there when she was scared or lonely. Every day on her way home from school, Kathleen feared that no one would be home when she got there and no one would ever come home again. She constantly feared that her mother was going to die. She was too young to understand that her mother and older sister suffered from an illness. She didn't realize that this illness was also why her dad had left. Like so many children in families with this level of dysfunction, Kathleen often thought that if only she were better, smarter, and more helpful, her dad would not have left and her mom would not be locked in her bedroom so often.

Her other sister and brother were as miserable as she was, and all three tried to escape the chaos of the home by hiding in their bedrooms or retreating to their neighbor's or their grandparents' houses. Seldom did they feel like a family. Instead, there was always lots of screaming, slamming doors, crying, and hardly ever a meal at the kitchen table with everyone present. She and her siblings would have missed meals on many consecutive days were it not for her grandparents. But because of them, she generally had clean clothes and an occasional reprieve from her dread about what was going to happen next at her house.

When Kathleen was in the last year of middle school, her mother went into treatment. Upon returning home, her mother still retreated to her bedroom. There was still very little discussion in the home, and many meals appeared at the kitchen table, but the alcohol and drugs were gone. Although Kathleen still never knew if anyone would be home when she got there after school, she gradually grew a bit less fearful that her mother was going to die or that everyone was would be gone, never to return.

▐▙▟▌

SHATTERED DREAMS

Even though her mother was finally sober, Kathleen's struggles were far from over. Even though her father had been out of their home for a few years, she had still seen him some weekends, when he was sober enough to make the trip to her town. On his last trip to see his children, he wasn't sober, and on the way, he had a car accident and was killed. Kathleen had always dreamed that one day he would come for her, and she would move away and have a new and different life. With his death, that dream was shattered.

She developed an eating disorder in high school, followed by a few bouts of alcohol abuse. While in college, she developed panic attacks and acute anxiety that landed her in the hospital and under suicide watch on more than one occasion. Her family was deeply troubled by her condition, but they were at a loss as to how to help her. Her mom, who was now very stable in her recovery, knew that Kathleen might have to live with her anxiety disorder for the rest of her life, just as she was living with the disease of alcoholism, but Kathleen would have to seek her own help for it.

Although Kathleen's condition was complicated by a multitude of fears, they were all intertwined in one basic fear: the fear of abandonment. As a young woman, she considered herself unworthy of love because she had never received the affirmation that she was a significant member of her family. She had been terrified, for so many years, that they would all leave and not tell her where they had gone. Occasionally her thinking was even more dire: they might intentionally not tell her where they had gone.

Living with this level of fear for more than two decades is deadening to the spirit. When Kathleen came into my life, I was acutely aware of how dim the light of her spirit was. She was seeking help for her struggle to feel worthy, but she had not yet made the commitment to doing the work that might be necessary to move from the "familiar" to a better place.

But she was already trying, on an incident-by-incident basis, to keep other people's actions or words from controlling her feelings. This behavior was a major shift for her. She had spent her lifetime letting whatever was said to her or around her determine how she was going to feel. She felt empowered almost immediately after learning that she could take responsibility for how she felt about or responded to situations, but she also found that it was not easy.

|‖‖‖‖|

A SENSE OF BELONGING

Through Adult Children of Alcoholics (ACOA) meetings, Kathleen has learned that she has a self-definition separate from the definitions that others around her have given her. She is not beyond being criticized, but she has learned that criticism usually defines the critic more than it might define her. Knowing this has given her permission to discard the put-downs. And being able to live free of others' criticisms and opinions gives her what she describes as a feeling of lightness. She had never fathomed she would feel free from chaos, free to be herself, free from anxiety most of the time, free to pursue interests that were hers and not someone else's. She says it's as though she has been reborn.

The progress that Kathleen is making in ACOA has also allowed her to relinquish her regrets over all she didn't have as a child. The hurt occasionally creeps in again, particularly if she has felt rebuffed by a friend or colleague, but she is able to rally by using the tools of her recovery program. No longer is she haunted by the sense that she doesn't fit in anywhere. She knows that in her ACOA group she not only fits but also has a story understandable to everyone present. She is also finding success in carrying that sense of belonging into many situations that would have terrified her in years past.

She has learned to remove herself from some situations, such as family gatherings, on occasion, particularly when she is not feeling strong. Staying away not only allows her fellow family members to resolve their own conflicts, but also allows her to avoid the anxiety that comes from trying to create a happy family. For too many years she was overwhelmed with the feeling that something crucial was missing from family interactions. She couldn't figure out what it was, but she assumed it was her fault. She now knows that wasn't true and that it isn't her responsibility to take control of any family situation or family member.

In addition, Kathleen has learned how to recognize when she is not healthily detached from a person or circumstance. When an attached feeling becomes apparent, she knows how to move her mind away from the setting and stop whatever her thoughts are incorrectly telling her. She has learned how to be disciplined with her thinking, her speaking, and her planning for the moments ahead, and that has saved her many times from feeling unfairly treated, one of the deadliest of all feelings.

Finally, she understands that she cannot will things to be different. She can and does choose to be with people who support her and love her unconditionally. She no longer feels guilt or thinks that she must change if she is not getting the reactions from others that she expected. Being detached, she says, means being her own loving parent rather than seeking acceptance from others for every action or feeling she has.

▐▞▞▞▞▌

INSIGHTS

With the help of ACOA meetings, counseling, and the program literature, Kathleen has changed her perspective on life dramatically, and she was eager to talk to me about what she has learned and now practices on a daily basis.

One thing she described is how having a set of spiritual beliefs for the first time in her life has helped her. These beliefs have lifted the angst that dogged her steps and her thoughts since she was a child. She believes now that there is some force guiding the course of her life. She celebrates the idea that she has the power to influence some details of that course, but she rests more easily knowing that her Higher Power is playing a crucial part. For the first time in her life, she can rest in the certainty that she is not the one in charge and that all is well. As Kathleen has discovered, even when we are in the midst of insanity and pain, God is waiting in the wings to lift our spirits and take charge of the outcome. All we need to do is agree to let go of our need to have that outcome fit our plan.

Letting our Higher Power be in charge of our life and everyone else's, too, at first may seem like a foreign and perhaps even irresponsible decision. In our American culture, we are told to be strong, to be independent, to need no one, to rely only on ourselves. When I was young, it seemed like turning to God for help was the coward's way out. I believed for years that only weak-willed people thought there was a God who had something to do with our lives. But, just like Kathleen, I discovered how much more peaceful life can be if we can "let go and let God." And being absolutely attached to God is what allows us, paradoxically, to detach from everyone else.

Kathleen also told me that the one thing she continues to think of every day as she is preparing to go to work is that the twenty-four-hour period ahead of her is all she needs to think about. Because she has learned to live just "one day at a time," coming home from work tired is now a thing of the past.

I understand how she feels, because "one day at a time" is a concept that continues to help me detach from life's problems. At first I was slow to accept the idea that everything took time and that I needed to go through only one twenty-four-hour period at a time. My mind had never considered residing only in the present moment. Like most of the friends I hung out with, I had read Ram Dass's book *Be Here Now* more than once, but what it was really about was way beyond my comprehension. My mind hovered over the hurts of the past and on the fringes of constant fear about the future. I'd never noticed a little spot between these two extremes.

Because our minds so easily slip into the past or the future, living one day at a time takes constant vigilance. To counter the habit of dwelling on any time other than the present, the first step is to notice when our minds are occupied with last year or next month instead of now. We can check for this tendency by simply noting what we are thinking about in any given moment. The second step is to gently remind ourselves, "Don't go there." At first, I had to repeat that suggestion to myself a few dozen times, but now saying it has become a good habit, as has living in the here and now.

Letting go of all of tomorrow and living one day at a time allows for a sense of real freedom. When we live in the present, we free our minds to gather the wisdom and information we need to actually be ready for the future, so that when tomorrow arrives, we will be ready for it.

CHOICES

ROBERTA'S STORY

ROBERTA WAS A RESILIENT CHILD. As one of four daughters in an alcoholic family, she began to look outside of the family for comfort while still very young. Because of their alcoholism, neither parent was emotionally available to offer her comfort or healthy, sensible guidance. Most of what she heard at home was criticism. Miraculously, she managed to shrug off this negative feedback, and she sought good feelings from success in school and elsewhere.

When Roberta was eight, her mother had a nervous breakdown. Roberta went to live with her aunt's family and thus discovered that there was another way for a family to live. Since her aunt's household seemed normal, at least as Roberta remembers it now, she used it as a measuring stick for how a happy family ought to be. Since her own family didn't resemble her aunt's family, she planned to imitate her Aunt Jean's life when she grew up and create a nuclear family that was like her aunt's.

Roberta realized at a young age that the farther away she was from her family, the better she felt. Like most people in alcoholic families, she began to isolate herself in the hopes of avoiding the wrath that was often routinely present at home. Even though she had three sisters, she wasn't close to them. She was studious and quiet and often alone in her bedroom. When her mother officially left the family while Roberta was in high school, it hardly affected her, since Roberta had grown accustomed to fending for herself.

In school, Roberta was a loner and not outgoing, but she also was a successful student and well-liked. The man who would become her first husband, Ben, was considered by everyone to be the most handsome boy in their class. Roberta and Ben made a beautiful couple; everyone said so. They were married right after high school graduation.

Unfortunately, the marriage couldn't be sustained after drinking became a part of Ben's daily routine. They had three daughters before divorcing. Roberta remained quite resilient, even in the face of a failed marriage. She seldom let her emotions get in the way of her drive to succeed. She wanted to set a far different example for her daughters than the one that had been set by her mother. She got her college degree after her divorce and became a certified public accountant. Before many years had passed, she had a successful career. She was an entrepreneur with a vision—not only about her career but also about the way a family should function.

┝┅┅┅┥

NEW RELATIONSHIP, NEW ISSUES

The struggle for healthy detachment wasn't an issue for Roberta until she became involved in a significant relationship with another alcoholic. Although Thomas was sober and in a Twelve Step program when they met, he had not progressed very far in his recovery. As a consequence, he was quick to blame Roberta, or anyone else who happened to be close by, for anything in his life that wasn't happening smoothly. For the first few months of their relationship, Roberta accepted his accusations. Even when she knew she was not to blame, she swallowed her feelings and let Thomas have his way. However, it wasn't long before she could see that absorbing the blame didn't relieve Thomas of the need to strike out at her. She could see that her way of handling him wasn't good for her or him.

At the suggestion of a friend, Roberta went to Al-Anon. She had gone to meetings briefly while still married to Ben but hadn't continued once they had divorced. She wasn't convinced she needed these meetings, but Thomas also wanted her to go, so she did.

Even though she had relinquished some of her needs to stay in the relationship, she became willing, with the help of the tools of Al-Anon, to look at what she was doing. She knew her own value system was being compromised, and her innate independence and resilience kicked in once again. Thomas had been used to women meeting his needs, and he had not expected that Roberta would ever quit adjusting her life to fit his. But to his surprise, Roberta left the relationship and never looked back.

I first met Roberta during her relationship with Thomas. We were in the same Al-Anon group. I noted from the very beginning that she seemed less invested in what others thought than the rest of us. Unlike most of the rest of us, she was used to meeting her own needs, and she could see no reason for staying in a relationship that didn't nurture her. I marveled at how able she was to stay focused, in most instances, on her vision.

It's probable that Roberta's experiences while growing up taught her how to distance herself from others when they disappointed her or were not able to be there for her. She experienced those same feelings again after leaving the relationship with Thomas. But being alone didn't disturb Roberta. She had a career she loved and three daughters who adored her. Self-imposed isolation had protected her so many times in her past, and the familiarity of it actually comforted her after her relationship with Thomas ended. Roberta enjoyed the company of men, but she did not look to them for emotional or financial support. She didn't doubt her worth as a woman if a man paid little or no attention to her, and because of this characteristic, she was a great role model for many of the women in our Al-Anon group.

Eventually Roberta quit going to Al-Anon meetings, but our relationship continued to flourish. It was in this next phase of our friendship that she and I got to know each other more fully. And it was during this time that she met and married the man who remains her husband.

INSIGHTS

One characteristic that defines Roberta is her drive to succeed. She doesn't consider relationships unimportant, but she does put her personal goals above all else. She doesn't succumb to the negativity or others' attempts to control her, nor does she put aside what she needs to do for herself in order to take care of someone else's feelings.

Without a doubt, her dedication to herself is an admirable quality, especially in our culture, where women are often praised for putting everyone else ahead of themselves. During my friendship with Roberta, my commitment to my life as a writer has been strengthened. I have learned that if I don't do what I need to do in regard to my profession, I feel unfulfilled. And when a feeling of lack of fulfillment sets in, so does ennui and discontent and irritability and blaming and criticism and judging and depression. Like Roberta, we can learn how to detach from the moods, the behavior, the pleading of others, by actually being more attached to our own hopes and dreams. Roberta never lost sight of where she wanted to go, nor did she let a relationship partner's wants keep her from addressing her own needs first.

Taking care of one's self respectfully and treating everyone else in the picture respectfully, too, allows everyone to move forward free of negative judgment. This working example of detachment deserves imitation. Even as a child, Roberta accepted that she cannot change another person, and she doesn't mind at all. No matter how many times she might have wished her mother drank less, it had no effect. She simply got used to walking away from those situations that didn't please her. This ability has sustained her through many decades of living.

Getting "trapped," as she puts it, is a decision, even though it might not seem like one. No one can trap you into doing what you don't want to do without your consent. Attachment, enmeshment, codependence—whatever we might call this dependence—is clearly a choice; it is usually a choice that is made out of fear, but a choice nonetheless.

Choices—that's the bottom line. What kind of choices do we want to make? Roberta learned to make pretty good ones when she was still a youngster. Many of us are still struggling to make good choices. But people like Roberta offer us examples that might help us shift our perception.

ATTACHING VERSUS JOINING

It might be said that Roberta was a natural at detaching. Or it might be said that her fear of intimacy, sown in her family of origin, taught her to isolate herself and to be self-focused—and that's not the same as making a healthy choice to detach. Although Roberta was a good role model for many of us at Al-Anon, she also didn't allow herself to be vulnerable or to need others. To me, this invulnerability can be as much a flaw as a strength.

Reciprocity in relationships strengthens them. Generally, this reciprocity occurs through the normal sharing of one's fears and failings and dreams. If you aren't in the habit of revealing your inner self to anyone else, it's hard to build a relationship that is intimate and sustaining. Superficial friendships are easy to make, but we need to have at least one person who knows *all* of us.

So how can we have healthy reciprocity and vulnerability in a relationship without being unhealthily attached and codependent? The key is to distinguish between "attaching to" and "joining with" others.

For simplicity, we can think of attachment as the opposite of detachment. In other words, attaching ourselves is akin to clinging to another person and letting that person decide what we should be thinking or saying or doing. Living this way is a death sentence for our soul. It removes our choices for doing the next right thing. We do not want to cling or be attached in this way.

However, we do want to join with other people. The difference is that when we join with others, we still allow them to have their own opinions, have their own set of values, and make whatever choices are right for them—all without feeling that we need to concur. Even more important, we allow them their choices without feeling that we need to disagree. We can mutually allow one another the freedom to be whom or what we need to be with absolutely no judgment. As a result, we do not feel controlled by people we choose to join with, nor do we feel the need to control them.

15

LEARNING TO LET GO

HARRY'S STORY

ALCOHOLISM WAS RAMPANT in Harry's family. Both of his
parents and many of his siblings suffered with the disease, as did
Harry. At the time we talked, he felt fortunate that his childhood family
had stayed intact even though the disease created havoc for them. He said
his mother could be credited with that, since she didn't drink while the
kids were young. The disease had not skipped her, however, and as the
kids grew up and learned to fend for themselves, she took her place at the
bar next to Harry's dad. For a number of years, they spent more time in
the bars than at home. After work each day, they'd meet there and drink
until closing. Day in and day out for years, the pattern didn't change.

Then Dad began to experience hallucinations. He fought with
people who weren't really there, at home and in the bar. He began to

beat up Harry's mom. On a regular basis, he'd lock himself in the attic and fight with the walls, the shadows, the imaginary creatures he'd swear were chasing him. Finally, after being diagnosed as a diabetic, he went into treatment for alcoholism. He didn't stay sober immediately after treatment and for a few years continued to smoke pot, but he has been drug and alcohol free for more than twenty years now.

Meanwhile, Harry's mom is traveling her own journey to sobriety, and it isn't over yet. Her drinking isn't like it once was, and she isn't always drunk. She has maintained her job as a schoolteacher on a reservation. But she isn't always sober.

Harry and his five siblings began drinking, too. Not unexpectedly, Harry also began dating women who drank. (Alcoholics generally gravitate to other alcoholics.) He didn't want to repeat the patterns that he had observed in his own home, but that was exactly what he began to do. Because he had often been the caretaker in his family when his dad got drunk and violent, Harry vacillated between taking care of the women he drank with and drinking abusively right along with them. One might say he was the classic codependent alcoholic. Loving to drink with the guys on his athletic teams and the women he dated seemed like the natural course for his life to take.

But eventually Harry began to tire of being the caretaker. When he met Adrianne, he thought perhaps he had met a woman who would help him chart a new course for his life. They became acquainted on a softball team. She was fun, a good athlete, cute, and a Native American like himself. Although she at one time had been a heavy drinker, at the time Harry met her, she had given up drinking. With her as a role model, Harry quit. He didn't discuss his quitting with Adrianne; he just did it. He was surprised at how easily he left the alcohol alone, because he knew quitting had not been easy for his dad. In fact, most people who had hung with Harry in the bars had quit drinking, again and again, only to return to it and the bar life. Harry, quite miraculously, never took another drink from that first day that he said no to beer after a softball game.

He and Adrianne played ball, hung out, and became very good friends over the next couple of years. Surprisingly, Adrianne had been a friend of Harry's dad for a couple of years before meeting Harry—another fact that impressed Harry. His dad didn't become friends with many women. All the signs looked good to both Harry and Adrianne, and their friendship moved to the next stage: intimacy. Adrianne became pregnant soon after they moved in together.

WHEN A SPOUSE RELAPSES

After their first child was born, Adrianne started drinking again. Harry was stunned and disturbed. He had never considered the possibility that she would drink again. He had been able to stop so easily, and the thought of starting again had never occurred to him. Why would it be any different for her? This relapse was the beginning of the roller-coaster ride. Adrianne would drink for a while and then get sober again. Over and over, the cycle was repeated. She even willingly went into treatment, only to return to drinking after a few months of sobriety.

When she became pregnant with their second child, she again quit drinking. They married, and Harry breathed a sigh of relief. He figured her latest recovery meant she had turned the corner and drinking would be a thing of the past, for good. Alas, that was not the case. Very soon after their second son was born, she began stopping at their old hangout after getting off work, and Harry had again become a caretaker. He was powerless to make her stop, but he didn't believe that he was. He tried in every way he could think of to keep her from drinking. She would stop occasionally, of course, but the reprieve was always short lived. The allure of the bars kept calling, and she kept answering.

Occasionally she was using drugs, too, including crack cocaine. Often she didn't show up to pick up their sons from activities. Sometimes she never came home at all, for days at a time. Harry's rage erupted often at her, and it would spill over to the kids. He just didn't understand why she couldn't put the drinking aside as he had done. Harry struggled with his powerlessness over what Adrianne was going to do next.

Because he'd been a caretaker in an alcoholic system most of his life, it was not easy for Harry to give up that role. Being the "good parent" had become one of his greatest assets. He was embarrassed by Adrianne's behavior, and he was tired of trying to explain to their boys what her problem was. They didn't understand about the disease; they knew only that she often did not come home, or when she did, she came home drunk. Harry often painted the picture of her drinking in even darker ways than was really the case because he was so mad at her for not stopping. He could see that the boys began to punish Adrianne in the same ways that they saw Harry punish her. He knew it was wrong, but he didn't try to stop it. His frustration was at a breaking point.

Harry's struggle to detach in a healthy way from Adrianne's unpredictable behavior was going to be a lifelong endeavor. It was finally evident to him that his attempts to control her would never meet with success, but his rage at her still took control of his life. His attitude, his willingness to understand about the severity of her disease, and his openness to getting help for their sons were often tainted by his disgust with Adrianne. He had stopped drinking so easily. Why couldn't she? He was tormented by that question.

|♯♯♯♯♯|

WHEN HOPE FADES

After years of trying unsuccessfully to get Adrianne to stop drinking, Harry finally went to Al-Anon at the suggestion of a friend. In my most recent conversation with Harry, he said that Adrianne had once again sought help for her addictions. He has given up being hopeful, though, and he has divorced her. He says he is done with trying to control her and is no longer even concerned with her struggle to be sober and drug-free.

What troubles him most right now is his sons' future. He doesn't want them to follow in their parents' footsteps, and he knows that, statistically, the odds aren't in their favor. He is curbing his comments regarding their mother, too, though it has not been easy. He had loved Adrianne very much, and he was deeply hurt by her inability to have a sober life with him. He knows alcoholism is no one's fault, and he is trying to help his boys understand that they didn't cause and can't change Adrianne's illness. Teaching this lesson is not easy for Harry, because his own history makes it hard for him to keep his anger in check when his frustration rises about how their lives have unfolded.

However, Harry has acquired a number of the tools of Al-Anon. He laughs a lot more now, he says. He also has been going to AA regularly. At the time of our last conversation, he appeared more peaceful than in any of the other discussions we've had.

INSIGHTS

Harry credits Al-Anon with allowing him to begin the process of letting go of Adrianne, although he recognizes how easily he gets sucked into trying to control other aspects of his life or the lives of others. He is trying to understand that *letting go* is more than just giving up trying to make another person do your will. His sponsor told him letting go means giving up even thinking about what the other person should do. He isn't there yet, he says, but he is moving in that direction.

As Al-Anon says so often to newcomers, "You didn't cause it, you can't control it, and you can't cure it." Harry seems to have finally accepted this truism. When I asked him what had changed most about his life since he got involved in Al-Anon, he said he no longer has the obsession to control others. Like most of us, he had never recognized that most of his behavior throughout his entire life was in reaction to what someone else was doing or saying. That he had a choice to act rather than react to the situations around him filled him with hope and enthusiasm about his future and the future of his sons.

Like Harry, many of us in Al-Anon joined this journey because of our addiction to controlling the many people, places, and situations in our lives. And, like Harry, we have learned the peace that comes from letting go of our need to control anyone other than ourselves. I remember reading the First Step at my first Al-Anon meeting and thinking, "I am not powerless over alcohol! John is!" I didn't hear the rest of the step. I simply didn't consider myself powerless in any way. If I put my mind to something, I could force it to happen—or so I thought.

Now, however, I glory in the fact that I am powerless over so much. Every person I spoke with for this book came into Al-Anon intent on changing someone else, generally self-righteously so. But by sticking around and listening at meetings, we learn, to our great relief, that changing someone is not our job, after all. It is not our job to be in charge of the outcome of any situation, either. The principles of Al-Anon shorten our job description significantly. I can't believe how much more peaceful my life is simply as the result of giving up my focus on my husband and others.

Fortunately, when we are willing, it becomes possible to make the decision to let go of others. The result is gratifying. Meeting rooms all over the world are filled with men and women who have made this decision. We cannot make so dramatic a change alone. The hope that Harry has now is the hope we can all be blessed with when we join with others who have traveled a path similar to our own, as he has done. Then, like Harry, we can experience the peace that we deserve.

16

A JOURNEY BEGUN IN YOUTH

JANET'S STORY

JANET, ONE OF THE LAST BORN of eleven kids, was easily over-looked in her family, or so she thought. The tension of living in a family with so many other kids, an alcoholic dad, and a severely codependent, religious mom, created unrest and innumerable fears for Janet. She never felt as though she belonged; one of her earliest memories was wondering if she had somehow wandered away from her "real" family and into another home. She still doesn't feel much connected to her siblings or her mother. They all existed side by side but with no strong sense of familial connection.

Janet's personal recovery story began when she was a teenager. From junior high on, she often escaped to the streets because of the tension and abuse in her home, and there she discovered drugs and alcohol. Her using friends seemed to give her life direction and meaning and give her "a family" to hang out with. The combination also gave her a bad attitude and a set of behaviors that would have led to serious trouble had it not been for an intervention.

She ended up in AA at the age of sixteen, ready to explode with anger, fear, and a sense of hopelessness. How could her life ever work out? she wondered. She met no one her own age for the first couple of years in AA, but she was taken in by the old-timers. She felt rather special, really. She had never had people her parents' age actually listen to her when she spoke. Nor had she ever considered that people *their* age had anything of value to say to her. The relationship that developed between Janet and the old-timers no doubt saved her life. In the same way that she had escaped to the streets in her early teens, she now escaped from her family by spending night after night at meetings.

Janet, now in her forties, has made a fulfilling life for herself. She was sober for a dozen years before she got married, and she and her husband now have two children. Her husband is not a recovering person; however, he has his own set of irritating behaviors that finally drove Janet to Al-Anon a number of years ago, and she is grateful to him for pushing her in this direction. She assumes, at this point in her life, that she might always feel separate from her family of origin, and she can tolerate that. But she does want to feel connected, in a healthy way, to her husband, children, and friends. Going to Al-Anon has given her the tools to make their home a healthy place. She discovered that "doubling up" with both programs makes sobriety all the more durable.

ᛁᚼᛁᛁᚼ

INSIGHTS
GIVING UP JUDGMENTS

Janet is an extremely loving, nonjudgmental woman. I told her this, and she laughed, saying she had been told in the early days of her recovery that if she didn't get over her constant judgment of others, she would never stay sober. We concurred that nothing destroys one's well-being more than even a single, tiny moment of negative judgment. Because she came into AA so young, she felt the need to compare herself with other women all the time. Comparisons like these generally become very judgmental and habitual.

Janet says having a sponsor kept her from letting the judgments destroy her sobriety, but for a time, they continued to feed her insecurities. She said after years of listening to others in meetings, she eventually came to believe that every person on her path is there by design for her growth. Embracing this idea finally allowed her to get free of her constant judgments. Janet believes we get exactly what we need in this life. From our comparisons we will learn how to grow from what we get. The next step for Janet was developing a feeling of gratitude for all of her opportunities to learn that someone new on her path, even one who was suffering, had something to teach her. Those people suffering in our midst give us opportunities to pray for them, thus strengthening our own ties to God. Janet is continuing to work on her gratitude.

▐▟▚▟▚▟▚▌

LETTING GO WITH LOVE

Because she didn't marry until after she had been sober a few years, Janet expected her marriage would be smooth sailing. How wrong she was! She has learned how controlling she can be. She has also learned how impatient she is when others don't succumb to her will. The principles of Al-Anon have helped her become adept at letting other people go at their own pace. This lesson has been extremely valuable in her marriage, because she and her husband are often not on the same page. She continues to learn the value of letting go of all situations and people who are not directly under her care.

Janet said it was not just learning how to let go, but learning how to let go *with love* that turned her life and her marriage around. I know how I can let go of people or a situation by making the decision to "not go there" when my mind begins to obsess about changing them. But not going there *with love in my heart* takes the process one step further. It's this additional step that makes the difference in our state of mind and in the tenor of the world we live in. It is what also helps in the healing of the world around us. Any time we can find peace in our lives, we contribute a sense of peace to the people who are around us.

When Janet talks about letting go with love, she put it in unique terms. She says, "To let go with love means allowing the other person their dignity." She believes that everyone must find his or her own way, and if at first they fail, so be it. This may sound harsh, but those of us in Al-Anon have grown to appreciate the awareness that each of us has only one life to live: *our own*. We can no doubt all remember days, months, or even years when we tried desperately to live others' lives for them, and that we were never successful. Failure didn't keep many of us from trying again, but we are lucky that we have learned, or are learning, that we don't have to keep trying.

It is so simple to let others be themselves if we make the decision to. What many of us fail to understand, particularly as newcomers, is that we may have to practice letting someone be over and over again, day in and day out. Understanding powerlessness happens in phases for most of us, and that may be good. We might not appreciate our powerlessness as much if we'd fully absorbed the idea the first time we were introduced to it.

"Until one gets good at letting go, you always believe that things will fall apart when you do let go," Janet says. "That won't happen. Things will not fall apart. Practice will convince you of this."

|┅┅┅┅|

INVITING GOD IN

One of the elements of Janet's journey is her spiritual program. She was raised Catholic, and, although she was wayward for a period of time, she has remained Catholic. She has made this part of her journey a priority and wants to share it with her husband and her sons. Her spiritual program is more than just Catholicism, however. Her daily life incorporates the spiritual tools she has gathered from more than thirty years of Twelve Step meetings. These tools are not counter to Catholicism, and they emphasize the way we look at the people and the experiences in our lives.

Al-Anon, AA, and every other Twelve Step program are based on a set of spiritual principles. These programs offer us the promise that we are not alone with our struggles, no matter how dire or overwhelming they seem. Help is never more than a thought away. It is always available by making a phone call or going to a meeting—or getting on our knees.

Janet is intent on accepting the idea that she is exactly where she needs to be and that God is her guide and caregiver. She knows that whoever is with her is exactly the person she is to reach out to next. She believes this is how the universe works and how God shows up in our lives. As long as she remembers that principle and acts accordingly, she says, she will be doing the work she was born to do. She wants to always remember to be the best copy of the *Big Book* she can be.

Janet has learned that she can do almost anything that strikes her fancy when she invites God into the experience. This idea isn't mysterious to those of us who wander into Twelve Step rooms, but it is a relatively unknown experience or realization to many.

Janet believes that one of our tasks as spiritually directed people is to share our message of hope and serenity as far and wide as possible. Sharing our message doesn't mean getting up on a soapbox. It can simply mean telling another person what our life was like, what happened, and what it's like now for us as recovering codependent people. We have learned, or are learning, that giving back is what teaches someone else what we have learned. Giving back also keeps each one of us mindful of the miracles that have happened and will continue to happen in our lives as long as we are willing to shift our perception.

Coming into the rooms of Al-Anon has offered Janet many miracles. She is a miracle maker and a miracle seeker. That she wandered into my life a number of years ago was no accident. Now that she has wandered into your life, too, consider it a blessing.

ENOUGH IS ENOUGH

SARA'S STORY

SARA HAD BEEN IN AL-ANON for eight or nine years—almost as many years as she'd been married to Bobby, an alcoholic. When I first met Sara, I was impressed with how much clarity she had about her life's purpose. She seemed to understand the dynamics of her relationship with Bobby clearly, also. She recognized that he was not the problem, despite his alcoholism. She had come from an alcoholic home, although her father had been sober for several years. Her mother had not sought help from any program for her own dys-function, and Sara often found herself fighting old tapes—habitual patterns of thought and behavior—from her childhood.

As a young girl, Sara had prided herself on being self-sufficient. She seldom asked for help from anyone, and she was a successful student. Spending long periods of time alone was the norm for her. She had an image of herself as an island, needing no one. She thought this independence made her special, and she was proud of herself. She got compliments from others, too, for being so able to handle her life with little input from others.

Sara and Bobby met while in college, at a time when Bobby was doing well in school and had great hopes for his future. They shared so many of the same interests that they seemed to be the perfect couple. They had both studied journalism in college, and he became a great teacher. And then they married. Their lives were smooth and joyful for many months after their marriage.

When it became apparent that Bobby was in need of help, they had already relocated from the college town where they met and were involved in their first professional jobs. Depression was the first symptom Bobby expressed. He lost his drive to succeed. Because he wasn't handling his teaching job, he was demoted. Not long after the demotion, he began to drink to assuage his shame.

Sara, on the other hand, was excelling in her job as a newspaper reporter. She even won a Pulitzer Prize in her first year for an article she wrote about poverty in their region. Many of their friends assumed that Bobby drank because he was embarrassed that Sara was doing so much better than he was doing. However, he claimed that he was proud of her, and Sara believed he was. She felt genuine concern for Bobby's struggles and was willing to help him in any way that she could.

He decided that they should relocate. Sara hated to give up her job but wanted to help Bobby succeed, so she agreed. As is typical in cases like these, the move didn't solve the problem. Bobby drank more, and Sara worked more. Their expenses increased, and the burden of covering them was beginning to fall on Sara's shoulders, since she had the better job of the two. Bobby simply wasn't able to teach or work in any job that gave him any pressure, so he became underemployed.

A NEW TERMINOLOGY

As Bobby's drinking escalated, Sara grew scared. She knew she did not want to live the way her mother had lived before her father had gotten sober. She started putting pressure on Bobby to get help. Without much of a struggle, he consented. Because his parents had both been alcoholics, he first went to Al-Anon. Before long, with help, he realized that AA needed to be his first priority.

Sara also took the opportunity to get involved in Al-Anon, too. When she went to her first meeting, the terminology she heard people using—*caretaker, codependent, sicker than the alcoholic*—made her uncomfortable. She felt that her own life was moving along successfully and she didn't want to change it. She wanted Bobby to change his life. However, after continuing to go to meetings, she began to think differently about what Bobby's responsibilities in their marriage needed to be, and she began to see more clearly how she needed to change, too. Although Sara hadn't talked much about Bobby in meetings, her sponsor, Madge, could see the signs of Sara's codependency and told her that it was time to take her focus off Bobby entirely.

Sara saw how she had become the competent caretaker when Bobby got his first demotion. She also saw how she had remained in that role every time he was bummed out because of a job loss or getting turned down for a job he had applied for. Before Al-Anon, he once went without work for one entire year, and Sara held their lives and finances together. After finding Al-Anon, she tried hard to give up doing for Bobby what he needed to do for himself. He had become so good at letting her be in charge that he was willing to lie back and do nothing but stay sober.

FOLLOWING HER TRUE PATH

With the help of Al-Anon's tools, her sponsor's guidance, and the suggestions of the counselor she and Bobby were seeing, singly and together, Sara made some decisions that she had not anticipated ever making. She said she had always thought she and Bobby "would turn the corner," but she could finally see how the old patterns were simply too hard to break. He had grown too accustomed to letting her decide everything for both of them, and she could see he needed to be responsible for himself. This realization gave her the courage to leave the marriage. She wasn't sure where her own path was leading, but she knew it did not include charting Bobby's path for him.

Interestingly, her focus on people other than herself has continued to be one of Sara's issues. Because defining themselves according to their interactions with other people is second nature to codependents, leaving her marriage doesn't mean Sara has escaped codependency. Leaving any relationship doesn't automatically lead to detachment. One can be just as attached emotionally after getting out of a primary relationship as when still in it. Physical proximity to or distance from the significant other has little to do with how entrapped one feels by the behaviors of another person. Like many of us in Al-Anon, Sara has discovered that leaving a relationship doesn't automatically lead to detachment. One can be just as attached emotionally after getting out of a primary relationship as when still in it, and distance from the significant other has little to do with how entrapped one feels by the behaviors of another person. Although Sara and Bobby divorced and she is making progress daily, she has to be vigilant about keeping her focus where it belongs: on herself.

Working hard to get clarity about her need to move on with her life has also given Sara the opportunity to look again at her family of origin. She considers her family extremely dysfunctional and does not see it as her role to help them change the way they relate to each other. Their pain is clearly theirs, she says. She is prepared to share her own path only if they ask her about it. She is out of the advice-giving business; Bobby was her last client.

Not having to control anyone else has given Sara real hope for a fun future. No longer is she charting anyone's path—she's not even charting her own as tightly as she once did. The unpredictability of many aspects of her life excites her. Having a journey that doesn't rely on anyone else or need to include anyone else, even though someone might want to accompany her for a while, has changed everything about the way Sara dreams about her future. She is on a single-minded quest to live in the moment. She says that for her, living in the here and now is the best way to stay detached from what others do.

Sara still has some fear. What helps her most is remembering that although she got to where she is today in a most unexpected way, that way was directed by her Higher Power. She is convinced there are no accidents.

▐▐▐▐▐▐▐

INSIGHTS
KEEP COMING BACK

"Keep coming back!" That statement is often made at the end of a Twelve Step meeting, in unison by all members, or from one individual member to another. Without exception, everybody I spoke with for this book, including Sara, said they were so grateful that someone had suggested not only that they should come back, but also that they should go to at least six meetings before making up their minds whether Al-Anon was able to help them or not.

When Sara first went to Al-Anon meetings, hearing other women reveal their feelings about situations and relationships in their lives made her both troubled and fearful. She didn't want to look closely at her relationship with Bobby. She couldn't remember the last time she had let herself feel any emotion openly and fully. She had learned when she was very young that it was better if she simply smiled in response to any situation and pretended that everything was always okay. She hadn't realized that this mask had become her permanent persona. She had become good at seeing only what she wanted to see, and she didn't know what looking would trigger. But after a few meetings, she realized that other people were sharing things she could relate to.

Like Sara, not many of us are eager to sit in a totally unfamiliar group of people and share what's on our minds. I am also glad I was told at my first meeting that I didn't have to say anything at all. I could listen for as long as I wanted to. It didn't take me long to start sharing, but knowing I didn't have to relieved me greatly. The anxiety I felt when walking into my first meeting was torturous. If I had felt that way every time, I would have found many excuses not to go again.

One of the blessings of Al-Anon, both Sara and I agreed, is that even if you don't want to change, if you don't even want to listen to what others are saying, as long as you keep showing up, the information shared registers and the inner voice begins to speak to you in a different way. You will find yourself beginning to change anyway. *God does for us what we can't do for ourselves.* That's one of the promises in the *Alcoholics Anonymous Big Book*, and it is true.

▌▙▟▐

CHANGING OURSELVES

The key fact that we discover when we seek help from the Al-Anon program is that the solution to our problem, regardless of how we have defined it, is never found through trying to change another person. The very first thing an old-timer will say is that *we are here for ourselves*—period. We can't change the other person, but we can change ourselves. This message Sara heard loud and clear.

Like Sara, most men and women who come to Al-Anon have been constantly managing, or trying to manage, the lives of others. What we eventually come to understand is that our obsession with the actions of everyone else allows little time to peacefully plan our own actions. Our lives are unmanageable, not because we don't know how to manage them, but because we have so little time to pay attention to our own lives when most of every day is spent trying to manage or thinking about managing the lives of others.

When we unhealthily attach to someone, we imprison not only ourselves but also the other person. Neither party is able to grow appropriately, or to contribute his or her special gifts adequately. *Attachment restricts both people. Detachment, on the other hand, blesses both people.* When we make a decision to allow others to have their own opinions and own set of behaviors, we are freed from the burden of being in charge of the outcomes of the events in their lives, and others are freed to pursue whatever is theirs to pursue. The greatest act of love we can offer others is freedom from our attachment.

Were it not for Al-Anon, most of us would have no idea how futile our efforts are when it comes to others. We'd struggle, incessantly, to make them do our will, only to have to give up in frustration when they returned to doing whatever we'd been trying desperately to break them of. Were it not for Al-Anon, most of us would still be seeking *the way* to do something different so we could count on a different outcome. As Sara said at the end of our interview, "How does anyone do life without Al-Anon?"

CHANGES

CINDY'S STORY

I HAD NAIVELY ASSUMED, before getting fully committed to Al-Anon and its principles, that a nondrinking spouse always left a marriage if the alcoholic partner didn't give up the drug of choice and all other chemicals. By the time I met Cindy, I knew this was not always the case, but still, when I met people who were "hanging in there," in spite of constant frustration and pain, I wondered what was wrong with them. Early on I even suggested to a couple of women that they should leave "the jerk." Now I can't believe I did that, but we see only what we want to see, and I wanted to see the men as the only culprits in these situations.

In a perfect world alcoholism wouldn't exist, or if it did, people would get help for it without resistance. But in this world there are many homes where one partner is still using drugs and alcohol in spite of the consequences for the family. In many of these homes, innumerable attempts have been made to change the alcoholic's pattern of behavior, with little or no effect. Cindy's family represents one such home. She helped me to understand that there is another way to use the principles of Al-Anon to stay in a marriage regardless of whether the alcoholic partner quits drinking or not. Her story is enlightening.

Cindy's family of origin certainly prepared her for the situation that has been recreated in her own nuclear family. Her father was an alcoholic who came from an alcoholic family. Her mother was manic-depressive and seldom able to meet Cindy's childhood needs. Her older sister mothered her, but she left home when Cindy was only eight. There was a great deal of clinical depression throughout Cindy's family, which resulted in a lot of conflict among family members. Cindy tried to be the peacemaker.

Neither of Cindy's parents gave her the sense that she was a worthy, wanted child. Both parents simply had too many problems of their own to provide her with acceptance and unconditional love. This upbringing set the stage for the neediness that has plagued her for much of her life. In school she was quiet, withdrawn, and overweight.

|₩₩₩₩₩|

CARRYING THE LOAD FOR OTHERS

During and after college, Cindy made a separate life for herself. Unfortunately, one of her hallmarks became carrying the load for others. She never really felt connected to others, so doing favors for them allowed her to feel that she was necessary to their lives. After college, she moved in with a man who matched her profile for giving and taking. The relationship certainly was not based on love but on financial and emotional convenience. It offered Cindy little; however, she turned over her power to this man, and he took advantage of her. One day, after a painful abortion, Cindy returned home to find him having a drunken party. She turned to Tom, a friend she knew through a social group she and her boyfriend belonged to. Tom was a steady, ready ear when she needed to talk about her feelings. Shortly afterward, she left her boyfriend, feeling she was reclaiming a part of herself that she had not valued for a long time.

It was a natural progression for Cindy to move in with Tom soon after leaving her former partner. They were already friends; a love of music connected them, as did his willingness to listen when she needed support. It wasn't until they moved in together that Cindy became aware of Tom's excessive drinking. However, after only a five-month courtship, they married.

One of Tom's struggles has always been the feeling that he doesn't measure up, even though, according to Cindy, he is a brilliant engineer. His parents are both extremely well educated, but Tom failed to graduate from college. Dropping out has always plagued him, and Cindy surmises that this is one of the reasons he has used alcohol to excess for a number of years.

Early in their marriage, Cindy could feel Tom pushing her away because of her neediness. She never felt confident in her opinions or her decisions. There were times she even found herself contemplating suicide because she felt so inadequate. One night, their marriage hit a crisis point. Cindy and Tom were at a party together, but when Cindy wanted to leave, Tom refused. The disagreement quickly escalated into a fight in which Tom threatened to leave the marriage if Cindy insisted he leave the party, so she backed off, again.

Cindy's fear of abandonment pushed her to call a friend. Fortunately this friend was in Al-Anon, and the two of them went together to

Cindy's first meeting. The hope Cindy felt while driving home after that meeting convinced her that there was a better way to live her life.

It didn't take many meetings for Cindy to see that she had been obsessed with the lives of others since childhood. The more honest she became, the more she was able to see that she had been leading others' lives for years. She had never considered that she was worthy of having a life separate from the lives of the people around here. Her role had always been to blend in and try to make everyone else more comfortable. This behavior was rooted in her family of origin, and she had carried it into every other relationship. Because she had received little positive feedback for her efforts, she felt compelled to try even harder. When she became fully aware that her entire life was focused on others, she was devastated. But the other women in Al-Anon told her she could change any behavior that she really wanted to change.

▸▸▸▸▸▸

POWERLESS, BUT MOVING AHEAD

Step One of the Al-Anon program, recognizing that we are powerless over the disease of alcoholism and behavior of others, got Cindy's attention quite often when she first started Al-Anon. She struggled with her powerlessness over Tom for a number of years. She felt that his drinking was a reflection on her and desperately wanted him to stop. Even though she knew and firmly believed that alcoholism was a disease, she felt rejected when he would drink rather than stay sober to spend a quiet evening with her. She took it personally on behalf of their son, too. She knew Boyd felt hurt when Tom failed to show up for an after-school event or was unavailable to help him with homework. By applying the Al-Anon principles,

Cindy learned to let go of these feelings, since they only made her feel more inadequate.

Cindy says one of the areas Al-Anon has helped her most with has been her decision to stay in her marriage, regardless of what Tom does about his drinking. One of the most important things Cindy has learned is that even though she can't get many of her needs met with Tom, she can get them met in other ways. She has learned this lesson with the help of the other women in Al-Anon, she says. She is confident that with the continuing help of the Twelve Steps, her sponsor, the meetings, and books on codependency, she can not only survive but also thrive in the marriage. She knows that love is a choice, just as surely as anger or fear or feelings of unworthiness are choices. She is tired of making choices that don't honor her, and she has the strength now to make those choices that do.

She is trying to help Boyd understand this concept of choices, too. He is already exhibiting signs of low self-esteem, and there are many battles at home between him and Tom. Cindy sees her son make many choices that ultimately hurt him, but she thinks if she can continue to model healthy choices, he will be able to choose some of his reactions and behaviors more carefully, too. It's very hard to see your child hurting, she said, and knowing that Boyd doesn't want to be home alone with Tom saddens Cindy a great deal. Yet she also knows that Boyd must learn to speak up for himself and that she can't fight his battles for him. She knows it is not her place to manage his relationship with Tom, even though she wants to. There is a fine line between helping and interfering, and she is working hard to determine what that line is. Having a firm belief in a Higher Power is offering her the clarity she needs.

Cindy says she has learned so much from her Higher Power. God has not let her down. She has also learned how to put God in all of her relationships, and they have all changed for the better. She says that when you see God in the people you are focusing on, you can trust that they will be okay; they will follow whatever path they need to follow, and where you meet will be according to the divine plan for both of you. Perhaps her parting words are the most important ones: "You can only really detach from another person when you recognize everyone is God in human form."

Cindy is a walking example of all that Al-Anon can do for a person and the peace that we are promised when we turn our will and our lives over to the care of our Higher Power.

┣┼┼┼┼┤

INSIGHTS
NEEDING TO BE NEEDED

Cindy was typical of many people I interviewed. Being needed by others was what made so many in Al-Anon feel valued. I certainly relate to that feeling. I used to clean the house for my boyfriend, cook, and do his laundry. I was quick to buy the booze whenever I feared he was about to make plans that didn't include me. If I provided the liquor, I felt certain I would not be left behind. I tried to cement our attachment by being indispensable. At that time I believed that to be detached meant that I would be forgotten. In time, I was forgotten anyway.

Doing favors for others is not wrong. Indeed, being helpful to members of our family or to friends we hold dear is not inappropriate. But taking an action on behalf of someone else so that he or she will be indebted to us is never a right action. Taking care of someone else's needs so that our needs are met or so that we feel secure or indispensable is never the right thing to do. This behavior keeps us stuck. It cements our unhealthy attachment to another. It imprisons us, and our growth is deadlocked. Giving it lovingly and willingly and freely is great; giving our attention as a way to control the actions of anyone else is never loving.

Cindy's constant attention to the needs, the whims, the behaviors of others, whether they were directed toward her or not, left her far too little time to pay attention to who she was. This had been true all her life, but, sadly, she had never noticed her own life as separate from anyone else's.

Codependency simply allows us no freedom to think for ourselves, to act on our own, to be separate in purpose, direction, or perspective. When we're overtly focused on an alcoholic or anyone else, we're reluctant to take new jobs, develop new hobbies, or make new friends. Being clearly attached, feeling almost connected at the hip to the other person, seems safe, familiar, expected, and valued to the codependent. And nothing will ever change for the codependent until, like Cindy, he or she decides that having a life of one's own is valuable and that that life is worth living.

A FAMILY DISEASE

As Cindy's story shows, alcoholism is a family disease. No one in the diseased family escapes the effects of it. Because of the way the members of an alcoholic family interact with one another, the disease touches each of the family members, even if only one person in the family is an active addict. Every action causes in someone a specific reaction, one that is generally meant to counter the original action. Back and forth the ball is tossed; round and round whirls the merry-go-round. Not until at least one person steps out of the circle, as Cindy did, is change a possibility. Only then will the family dynamic begin to change.

At first, Cindy felt very tentative about trying any of the new behaviors she learned in Al-Anon at home. She was afraid that Tom might feel ignored and get mad at her. She was also afraid that he cared so little and drank so much every night that he might not even notice that she was reacting in a new way to the twists and turns in their relationship.

The first change she instituted was not to argue with him at night, particularly when he was drinking. No matter what he said or did in reaction to her, she gave no response when his comment was mean or argumentative. The first few times she tried this reaction, she felt almost giddy. The realization that she could choose to do something different from what she had been doing for years astounded her. And it was so simple! She just kept her mouth shut when it seemed he was trying to bait her into an argument with him. Walking quietly out of the room rather than responding to his jabs gave Cindy a new sense of her potential as a human being. She now understands that his attacks are about him, not her. She never understood this dynamic before coming to Al-Anon, and that profound realization has helped her live a better life.

While it is true that no one can control or change another person, it is also true that interactions will change when one person quits doing what he or she has always done. Cindy is living proof.

ᚼᚾᚾᚾᚼ

THE REALITY OF RELAPSE

Familiar patterns are hard to walk away from, even when they are very painful. Relapse is a reality for codependents just as surely as it is for alcoholics. Some may think relapse is not as dangerous for the codependent as for the alcoholic, since codependents will generally not be driving drunk or fighting violently with another person. But emotionally, a codependent's relapse is every bit as devastating. It instantly revives those old feelings of insecurity and unworthiness.

Cindy says she still falls back into her old behaviors on occasion. That's when she needs to HALT, as it is known in AA: to check whether she is hungry, angry, lonely, or tired, because at those times she is particularly vulnerable. Those of us who have been around the meeting rooms of Al-Anon for a while know how dangerous any of these shortfalls can be. If our reserves are low, we will revert to the old, familiar ways. On the other hand, Cindy knows that when she is taking good care of herself, getting enough sleep, eating right, exercising, getting to meetings, and so on, she is able to let Tom's behavior slide right by. Taking care of her own needs helps her practice healthy detachment and keeps her from slipping into old behaviors.

Codependency is seductive and extremely slippery. We can find ourselves caught in its web almost before we realize what we are doing. Being vigilant against it is a full-time job when we first become aware of it as one of our "natural" behaviors. Fortunately, when we are a part of Al-Anon, we are among friends who will show us the way to let go.

WORKING THE TWELVE STEPS:
STEPS ONE TO THREE

The Twelve Steps serves as a blueprint for building a new set of behaviors, and this blueprint offers hope that is so desperately needed when one seeks help for the problem of alcoholism in a friend or family member.

When I attended my first meeting and heard the Twelve Steps read, I had no idea we were expected to "work" them. I remember thinking that all I had to do was think about them and then live my life differently—automatically. I was used to mastering a set of ideas or a philosophy by simply studying an assigned essay.

Was I in for a surprise! When I heard men and women talking about their struggle to work one step or another, I was lost. I was embarrassed to let my sponsor know how little I understood, but she caught on. She suggested we begin working the steps together. That suggestion was crucial to my getting on track with the program. She helped me understand how to recognize my powerlessness and unmanageability. We covered each step in turn, and now I do the same helpful exercise with my sponsees, too.

STEP ONE: We admitted we were powerless over alcohol—that our lives had become unmanageable.

In Step One, we are reminded that we are powerless over alcohol, thus the alcoholic, too. This powerlessness means that we cannot change the alcoholic. We cannot cure them. We cannot control them. And it's not just the alcoholic that we can't change or control. We can't change or control any person in our life unless they have decided to let us be in charge of them.

Step One also asks us to recognize the unmanageability of our lives. For most codependents this is a bitter pill to swallow. Didn't we do our own work and still manage to cover for the alcoholic? How about all of the situations that we handled entirely alone, day in and day out? Taking on extra work wasn't unusual for many of us. We wanted to be noticed for our efforts. We needed as much approval from others as we could garner. It's not easy to understand how our lives could be considered unmanageable when we had as many balls in the air as most of us were juggling.

This part of Step One was very hard for me to admit to. I had a full-time teaching job at a university, was a straight-A graduate student, and had a busy social life. Unmanageable? My life?

What had not occurred to me was that parts of my life were unmanageable. My emotions, for example, ran my life. I did not take charge of them. When anyone, anywhere interacted with me, I let the tenor of that experience decide how I would feel and thus perceive myself. With the help of a sponsor I was finally able to see this habit and then move on Step Two.

STEP TWO: [We] came to believe that a Power greater than ourselves could restore us to sanity.

Step Two says we can believe that there is a Higher Power whom we can turn to. Letting an unseen Higher Power take over all of the details we thought we were handling so well may seem like a desperate measure that has little chance of success. And the reference to "restoring our sanity" may seem ridiculous to some newcomers. It may have never even crossed our minds that our incessant, obsessive need for control was insane. We were only doing what we had to do, after all. Were it not for this step, very few of us in Al-Anon would ever define our behavior as insane.

But relief awaits us when we finally do say, "Yes, I was insane in how I was living my life and trying to live others' lives, too." What is even better is that we never need to return to that former state of mind. Insane behavior can be a description of our past and only our past.

STEP THREE: [We] made a decision to turn our will and our lives over to the care of God *as we understood Him.*

I personally had no spiritual belief system before coming to Al-Anon. I didn't know spirituality was part of the "education" when I got to the program, so it didn't much affect me one way or another. I simply went along with the ritual of the opening and closing prayers. I heard God being mentioned in many of the talks and the Twelve Steps, but I didn't absorb the information. I didn't think the "God stuff" would hurt me, but I didn't consider it vital to being able to get more control over my life and the people in my life. What was vital was my need to feel less anxious and more in control.

The paradox, of course, was that when I eased up on my resistance to letting God in, my anxiety lessened. The presence of my Higher Power, which had been there all of the time, was the antidote to the turmoil that was the center of my life. To get this payoff, all I have to do is be there, in that presence. I don't have to do anything but show up and listen with my heart and mind. I am actually grateful that I found God elusive at first, because that elusiveness kept me coming back.

Step Three is considered by some to be the most important step of all. I remember hearing an old-timer at an AA meeting say that if we were having any problem in our life, any problem at all, we had not done Step Three. Letting God be the absolute decision maker in our life takes away the guesswork, the anxiety we might have about the decisions we think we have to make, the confusion about the future that so often troubles us. Nothing seems hard about any detail of the impending day's activities if we allow God to be in charge.

Giving up control of the details of our own life and all of the people in that life is not a onetime decision for most of us. I was so relieved when I heard that same old-timer say we must do Step Three again and again, maybe even many times in a single day. This knowledge makes it possible to start the process of "turning it over" as many times as necessary.

Step One, Step Two, and Step Three set the stage for a profoundly different life experience. If we were to do none of the rest of the steps, we would still realize significant rewards on a day-to-day basis. But fortunately, most of us don't stop with the first three.

19

REVISING EXPECTATIONS

NORA'S STORY

N ORA HAS BEEN SOBER for more than two decades. Neither of her parents was an alcoholic, but the behavior consistent with an alcoholic setting was prevalent in her family nonetheless. No doubt there were alcoholics throughout the family tree. Among her siblings, alcoholism has paid its respects. One of her sisters, Sylvie, is a "sometimes sober" alcoholic and drug addict but without a program. Her other sister, Rae, has chosen to be separate from the family.

Nora began drinking while in college and discovered alcohol made her less uncomfortable around others, particularly men. It wasn't long before she was drinking daily. She gravitated to men who were daily drinkers, too, of course, and married the first one who proposed.

The marriage soon unraveled, but not before a son was born, a son who in time followed in his parents' footsteps. But Nora did get sober. Her life wasn't very stable, however, until she sought the help of Al-Anon after her son became troubled by alcohol and other drugs. When he went into treatment for his dependence, she went to Al-Anon for help. She was not certain what she would learn there. Having been in AA for a number of years by that time, she wasn't sure she needed additional help. So many of us who finally wander through the doors of Al-Anon ask, "Isn't one program enough?" For Nora, the answer was no. She went to Al-Anon to find help for parenting an alcoholic son, but what she found was help for reparenting herself.

What Nora realized after going to Al-Anon was how dependent she was on men to make her life meaningful. AA had definitely helped free her from her dependency on alcohol, but it had done nothing about freeing her from her dependence on men. She had never noticed how attached she was to the attentions, good or bad, of the male figures in her life. The fact that they decided for her how she felt had gone completely unacknowledged until in Al-Anon meetings.

Today, Nora still is not as quick to leave relationships with significant men when doing so would be good for her. Slipping back into the persona of someone who meets another's needs rather than her own, if the other person is responding to her sexually and affirmatively, is far too easy for her. She knows her acquiescence relates to how she is feeling about herself at the time the "invitation" has been extended, but having the knowledge doesn't always keep her from holding back when she should. However, most of the time, Nora can and does walk away from unhealthy relationships when the need arises.

The self-esteem issues that haunted Nora in her youth before, during, and after her marriage, and within her significant intimate relationships since then, still need her attention, and perhaps they always will. These issues are weighty ones for many of the people

I spoke with, both men and women. Like Nora, many of us were deceived as youngsters into believing we were unworthy, stupid, ugly, troublesome, or too ordinary to ever count in the life of someone else. Learning that this was never true doesn't immediately rewrite the script in our minds. Al-Anon will help us rewrite that script, however, just as it is helping Nora.

Although her son and daughter were raised around Al-Anon for much of their lives, this fact didn't prevent them from struggling with alcoholism. But it does mean the solution for handling the disease is not completely foreign to them, and, as Nora looks over her whole life up to this point, she is most grateful for that.

INSIGHTS
LEARNING TO WALK AWAY

One of the first ways Al-Anon helped Nora was by giving her the strength to walk away from her family of origin when they treated her badly. Her estrangement from them was a long one, but she was present for her parents when they were dying.

Nora has often had to move away from her son, too. After her divorce, she had to send him to live with his dad for a time, since his behavior was beyond her control. She still has had to be away from him on occasion because he isn't consistently sober. This separation is hard for Nora, as it is for any parent in a similar situation. Moving away, both physically and emotionally, from individuals who at one time were significant to our development is never easy. But Nora believes that her son has a Higher Power in his life that is every bit as powerful as the Higher Power in her own life. And she knows his Higher Power is not her. She has the strength to stand back from his life and let him lead it his way regardless of what she may have hoped he would do. That same knowledge has also enabled her to give up her need to have her sister Sylvie work a recovery program similar to her own.

Nora has learned that once we accept that everyone has his or her own Higher Power, we can give up the responsibilities that we have unsuccessfully struggled with. We can also be more present to the little joys that were always coming our way but that we were too busy to notice. As Nora put it, "Detachment is a gift for both people. It acknowledges that the other person can take care of himself or herself and frees me to simply live my own life."

Nora says that being able to give up her expectations of what her kids need to be, what her ex-husband needs to do, or what her relationship with her own siblings needs to be has been the most fruitful aspect of the program. Expectations, like those that had ruled her life, are a setup for disappointment. Now, instead of letting her expectations define her perspective, she lets her perspective define her expectations. She knows that if expectations of others are not being met, she needs to change what she is looking for.

LETTING GO OF ANGER

Another thing Nora has learned from Al-Anon is to not let anger get the best of her anymore. The simple tool of counting to ten before reacting has saved her from many unnecessary arguments and embarrassments, because it allows her to step back and reconsider the value of making a specific retort. Waiting ten seconds can also give her a chance to seek another perspective on whatever has just occurred. (Personally, I have found that my Higher Power is always waiting for me to ask for another perspective about whatever has not met with my approval.)

The first thing we generally do when some things don't go our way is to look for the culprit and then give him or her a piece of our mind. The other person then has to address our reaction in some way. Getting angry, or attacking back when someone gets angry with us, never accomplishes anything. It only escalates a no-win situation for both parties. The instant gratification we think we will feel after returning a verbal assault is just that, a mere instant's worth of "gotcha" feelings. Then the shame sets in, and the argument has been elevated to a new level. Nora has discovered that the freedom not to be angry, regardless of what is happening around us, is a breath of fresh air.

WORKING THE TWELVE STEPS: STEPS FOUR AND FIVE

STEP FOUR: [We] made a searching and fearless moral inventory of ourselves.

STEP FIVE: [We] admitted to God, to ourselves, and to another human being the exact nature of our wrongs.

Step Four is about listing all of our transgressions. People who come into Al-Anon often mistakenly believe, at least initially, that they are not transgressors. I certainly didn't think I was. The first time I tried Step Four, I wrote a seventy-eight-page long, detailed account of what every person, particularly men, had done to me throughout my lifetime. I can remember feeling elated about getting all of this from my head, where it had been for years, onto paper.

I made the appointment to do Step Five with a clergyman who was also in Al-Anon. For more than four hours I read what I had written and he listened, seldom commenting. After the last page, I looked at him, expecting applause. He quietly and politely said, "Your inventory was about others, not you." I was confused, stunned, and hurt, and I felt like a total failure. I walked home and vowed to never mention this experience at a meeting.

Although I have never heard another person share a similar story at an Al-Anon meeting, I am sure that there have been others in the program who were unable to see their own transgressions when attempting Step Four for the first time. I grew up in a family where blaming was common, so I was very comfortable foisting responsibility off onto others when anything I was involved in went awry. I had played the victim so long that I couldn't imagine that I wasn't, in fact, a victim. The thing I had least expected from this step when I first did it was that it would so empower me in due time. It is the step that has had the biggest impact on my behavior.

What I finally learned, with the help of a sponsor and a lot more meetings, was that I couldn't get well unless I took responsibility for myself and the part I played in every interaction with others. Taking responsibility for every part of our lives, for the ugly parts as well as the ordinary and good parts, is what helps us become willing to change, with God's help, whatever behavior needs to change. Voicing that responsibility to God and to another person is what helps us truly surrender our resistance to letting other people know who we really are. Only then can we allow ourselves to be helped by people who have walked and are walking the same path.

I have found that doing Steps Four and Five additional times has been valuable. The further away we get from the past, the clearer some of it becomes. Also, the longer we are around other recovering people and the principles of the program, the more honest we are able to be.

HOPE REVISITED

BETH'S STORY

BETH DESCRIBES HER FAMILY of origin as ordinary. Her mom's father was alcoholic; although Beth's mother had some classic symptoms of being the adult child of an alcoholic, she showed no signs of alcoholism herself. Beth's dad traveled a lot in his work, and the family, as a consequence, moved often. Her parents were not abusive to one another or to the six kids. Home life was generally very respectful, Beth said. For the most part, they looked like the normal family. The main dysfunction was that everyone got involved in each other's business. The phone lines between Beth and her siblings ran hot most of the time after she left home.

Beth was the oldest of the children and from earliest childhood showed signs of being the great caretaker. She wasn't a child who got into trouble. She could always be counted on to do her part and then some.

In her family of origin, the only person who has shown signs of alcoholism is a sister, but Beth married a man with the disease. She and Brad met where they both worked, and she quite adeptly transferred her caretaking from her family to him. Naturally he was willing to accept the help. He had the classic hard-luck story, and she became the classic codependent. By the time they had small children, one of whom was in need of many surgeries, Brad lost his job. Beth sought the help of one of his friends, who helped her convince Brad to go to treatment.

Beth was both relieved and afraid by Brad's recovery. It scared her to not be in control of the changes that his treatment was likely to bring. Brad's counselor recommended that Beth go to Al-Anon. She wasn't happy about a counselor thinking she needed help. She figured she had been the one to make their lives work relatively well and couldn't see that she had a problem that needed fixing. But she was used to following what "authorities" said, so she went.

After Brad got out of treatment, he showed signs of growing up. His assuming some of the responsibilities he had shirked for so long took Beth by surprise, and she couldn't let go of her need to control these responsibilities easily. Her focus was on him after he came home from treatment. Her trust in him was low, and he could sense it. She felt justified in her feelings, but she could also see how they were keeping the two of them separate. She also knew that having a sick child meant they needed to be partners more than before Brad got sober.

For a while, Brad stayed committed to his program of AA, and Beth went to Al-Anon. Then he decided he didn't need the meetings any longer, because he was sober and working again.

|+++++++|

REFRAINING FROM SAYING, "I TOLD YOU SO"

One of the common themes that runs through the head of the codependent is, "I have done so much to keep this relationship alive and working! How dare you not do your part!" For ten years, with the help of Al-Anon, Beth struggled with this feeling, and for ten years Brad stayed away from meetings. However, because of a crisis with their chemically dependent son and their subsequent short separation, they went to a counselor. To Beth's gratification, the counselor suggested that Brad go back to meetings. Refraining from saying "I told you so" took some effort on her part. And, while Brad ignored the counselor's suggestion, it was also an effort for her to not remind him of what the counselor had said. Beth had so often felt alone in her dealings with the kids. For nearly ten years she had been holding up her end of the bargain, with the help of Al-Anon, never giving up hope that Brad would one day surrender.

Finally, with no specific prodding from her, Brad returned to AA, and he began to change. Beth could hardly believe it at first. She was a bit suspicious, in fact. Would it last? she wondered. But she decided to reap the joy of living in the moment and trusting God to take care of the tomorrows. Al-Anon had introduced her to this idea years ago, and now she could actually use it. She and Brad began to discuss their family problems. She began to feel as if they had a partnership after all, and loving their son, who continued to use, became a bit easier.

Beth realizes that were it not for Al-Anon, her family would have split up long ago. She would not have been willing to tolerate living with a dry drunk for as many years as she did without the help, wisdom, and patience that she garnered at every meeting. Al-Anon taught her what it meant to have her own life in spite of not having the life she had hoped for with Brad. With the help of her friends in Al-Anon, she committed to an exercise program, took time for play with friends, started each day with quiet meditation for herself, and did not let the behavior of her kids or Brad make her doubt her own value. That last point was perhaps the most difficult and the most important. Caretakers, as a matter of course, put others first. Putting herself at the top of her own caretaking list took an effort on Beth's part.

Beth says she can point to many areas of her life that have benefited from her commitment to Al-Anon, including her husband, her family of origin, and her colleagues. Pretty much everything about her has changed, she said. She no longer has to take responsibility for getting work done that is not hers to do. She doesn't have to keep score when others aren't holding up their end of the bargain, at home or work. Because of her work in the health-care field, she used to struggle doing for patients what they needed to do for themselves. She is free of that caretaking habit now. But best of all, she can lovingly wish her son, who is still using drugs, a good day and let him have whatever day he and his Higher Power are destined to have.

Knowing that her son's journey is indeed his has allowed her the kind of freedom from worry that she never imagined. It had never been her experience to feel peaceful before her recovery in Al-Anon. She had never known what peace might feel like or whether it was something even worth seeking. But she had gotten a taste of it on occasion over the previous fourteen years, and she knew she wanted more of it. Her sponsor told her she could get it in only one way: by surrendering her life and the life of her loved ones to God.

Little by little, experience by experience, she let go of everyone and everything. And peace came. But like with all newfound feelings, it's hard to trust that peace initially. And the codependent often goes back to old, familiar behavior. Beth did. However, she never forgot the formula for peace, and she returned to it again and again, until now it is the decision she knows she can trust the most. She is happy she no longer lives on the roller coaster of feelings that were her life for so long.

INSIGHTS

Beth still has her mini-relapses, when she begins to do for others what they need to do for themselves or she feels judgmental when something isn't being done her way. However, she catches her behavior quickly and reminds herself that Al-Anon is a program of progress, not perfection. She also knows it's a program of attraction, not promotion. Although she recognizes many people in her life who could gain a new perspective and greater happiness if they went to Al-Anon, she does not tell them they need to attend. She simply continues to attend meetings in the hopes that these others might say, "You seem different. What are you doing?"

One of Beth's techniques for staying detached is a visualization. When Beth feels a drama about to unfold, she sees herself standing off to the side, away from the fishhook that is being tossed in her direction. Rather than getting snagged by it, she steps back. She uses this visualization with her kids and with others who want to suck her in emotionally. With it, she can look on her kids or others with love and walk away, unhooked. And she feels no guilt. That's the real reward.

"Clean relationships" is the term Beth used to describe those interactions that are most common to her now. She knows that detaching doesn't equal a lack of love. It equals, in fact, greater love. Letting someone else be whoever they need to be, whether that's the person we hope they'll be or not, is what's right. We think we should be in charge of another's journey only because we fear that their journey might take them away from us. But if it does, so be it. I remember hearing many years ago in the fellowship that God never removes from our lives someone who still needs to be in our lives. I am convinced of this truth.

Beth said the best part of her journey has become those moments when she and Brad sit down together to use the principles of the program to make decisions about their lives as a family. They want to be on the same page. She had never dreamed they would reach this point, and now it seems so natural. Willingness is the essential factor. That's really all it takes for any one of us to make a significant change in our lives. Our Higher Power will do the rest, just as we have been promised. God is now and has always been waiting to do for us what we can't do for ourselves, and Beth says, "It's time to let Him."

Living with a dry drunk is no different from living with an active alcoholic. The behavior is similar. The attitude is similar. And the remedy is similar: take charge of what you want to do and say, and do and say only that. We never have to let the behavior of anyone else decide what our behavior needs to be. As Beth knows, if we are willing to take responsibility for ourselves, we will get the power we need from "the One who has all Power," and that power will enable us to be who we really want to be.

WORKING THE TWELVE STEPS:
STEPS SIX TO NINE

STEP SIX: [We] were entirely ready to have God remove all these defects of character.

STEP SEVEN: [We] humbly asked Him to remove our shortcomings.

Steps Six and Seven are closely aligned with Steps Four and Five, but I didn't realize that for some time. I was very lax about seeking any kind of help from my sponsor; I didn't want her to know how little I knew. I have to laugh at this now, but it was painful and oh, so true back then. Steps Six and Seven are commonly referred to as the forgotten steps. Because Steps Eight and Nine address what has been uncovered in Steps Four and Five, it's perhaps not unusual for people to skip over Steps Six and Seven. But they are just as crucial for the codependent as any other of the steps.

Step Six asks us to be entirely ready to have our defects (as outlined in Step Four) removed. In Step Seven we ask God to remove the shortcomings. What we need to understand is that we are not expected to remove them on our own. Doing nothing on our own is one of the biggest changes most of us need to make after coming into the Al-Anon fellowship. Most of us are used to doing so much alone, not only those things we needed to do but also those things others needed to do for themselves. These two steps quite clearly tell us to do all things with the help that has been offered.

Those of us who share this program become willing to give up our attempts to control everyone else. We decide that belief in a Higher Power greater than ourselves makes sense. In fact, we try to seek that Higher Power's guidance on a frequent basis. We become willing to be more responsible about our past and present. We go to God to admit who we really are. And we ask for God's help in freeing us from those behaviors that made our lives miserable in the past. This adds up to a lot of change.

STEP EIGHT: [We] made a list of all persons we had harmed, and became willing to make amends to them all.

STEP NINE: [We] made direct amends to such people wherever possible, except when to do so would injure them or others.

When my sponsor and I first worked Steps Eight and Nine together, she made a point of telling me that these two steps were no less important to my serenity than all the rest of them. I was certain that an alcoholic needed to attend to these steps more than I needed to. I truly didn't think, for my first three months in Al-Anon at least, that I had harmed any one. When my sponsor suggested I had harmed myself, at the very least, I finally became willing to agree, but even that idea seemed strange to me.

It was not until I heard Step Eight discussed a couple of times at meetings that I got a glimmer of the harm I had done to myself and others. Any codependent has harmed him or herself without a doubt. It harms us to put our own needs at the bottom of every list of what needs attention. Eventually I could see how I had never listed my own needs. I could see how my dance had always been around someone else's life.

What my sponsor also helped me to see was that dancing around someone else generally meant I was actually taking the lead for that person. Taking the lead, in turn, meant I was making another person my hostage, not allowing that person the freedom to assume responsibility for his or her life. Anyone I had done this to had been crippled by my actions. While it's true that others could have rejected my efforts, I still had to be accountable for my part in the dance. Steps Eight and Nine would make me accountable, my sponsor said.

What I did not realize when we first began working Steps Eight and Nine was how significantly different my relationships with the harmed people would become when I took responsibility for my part in whatever the struggle was. I was not in the dark about how tense many of my relationships were, but I didn't know that my feelings would change as a result of simply making amends, in the form of an apology, for my part in our relationship's tension. I had never dreamed how pleasant and loving my relationships with many significant individuals in my family and beyond would become.

Before making amends, I had to put the person's name on my list. The miracle began at that point. People who I hadn't acknowledged, maybe not even seen for some time, but who had been hovering in the back of my mind, began to reappear in my life as soon as I scribbled their name on my list. My sponsor said God called them forth. All I had to do was show some willingness to do what I needed to do, and God opened the door for my growth. Steps Eight and Nine changed every feeling I had about my family of origin, for example. My parents and I became loving friends and confidants, all because I took responsibility for my behavior, which had caused such turmoil in our family. It didn't matter that at one time I had dreamed that they would apologize for what I considered were their transgressions. My resentments were gone just as soon as I made my amends. The good relations with them continued until their deaths.

This program, one part of it or another, will change a person's life beyond their wildest imagination. Every person I spoke to for this book, every person I hear speaking at any Al-Anon meeting I attend, is a living testament to this fact. We leave every meeting a little bit changed. Regardless of which steps we have completed and which are still waiting, we are in the process of change and we have a lifetime to do it.

LETTING GO

CAROLYN'S STORY

CAROLYN HAS BEEN IN RECOVERY for her codependency for nearly three decades. She was raised in a relatively functional family. There was no active alcoholism, but her dad expressed a lot of rage, and her mother played the always-willing victim. Because of her mother's codependency, Carolyn learned some unhealthy behaviors that troubled her parents. She, too, willingly let any attention from a male dominate her behavior. That's how it was when she met Sam. He was a rebel and very exciting; she was shy and very introverted. They were made for each other, Carolyn says laughingly. He was already drinking when Carolyn met him, and she followed him everywhere, working to meet his every demand.

His every wish was her immediate command. Every choice she made had him in mind. Every mood he had she attempted to mimic or assuage. He was often angry. It was the alcohol that triggered his anger, but she was always certain it was something she had done. Consequently, she worked extra hard to change his mood so he wouldn't leave her. She had no idea she had given up her life to be his extension, to be whatever he wanted her to be on a moment's notice, but she had. Having an identity of her own seemed unimaginable and even threatening, because if she did maybe he wouldn't want her.

They married right out of high school and began their family. Their passion for each other was embarrassingly evident to everyone in their lives. So was Sam's drinking problem. Carolyn could see it too, but she could ignore it if she was drinking with him. This is what she chose to do for the first few years of their marriage.

Then the problems that occur in any alcoholic family began to happen. Sam couldn't hold a job, and Carolyn became the primary wage earner. Sam got into fights that Carolyn had to retrieve him from. He had many accidents from drinking and driving, and Carolyn kept bailing him out of jail. Her own drinking made it extra hard for her to hold the family together.

Fortunately, one of her sisters confronted Carolyn and said she would see to it that Carolyn would lose the children if she didn't get help for herself and Sam too. This turning point was the beginning of the journey into recovery for both Carolyn and Sam. The first step for Carolyn was that she quit drinking. About six months later, Sam did the same.

Next Carolyn went to Al-Anon, where she heard the term "codependency." She knew immediately that its definition fit her behavior to a T. But she had no idea what to do with this new knowledge. How else could one behave? she wondered. Slowly and with the help of a sponsor, Carolyn began to see that it was possible to choose behaviors that were different from those she had grown accustomed to. However, when she did, Sam immediately reacted and mistrusted what she was learning in Al-Anon. He felt threatened, fearing that Carolyn's program was going to break up their marriage. There were times when Carolyn wasn't so sure that it wouldn't.

NEW PERSONAL POWER

Carolyn was quickly learning how to take care of herself. She did a lot of backsliding, she says, but nonetheless, she did respond from a position of personal power that Sam had never seen. Fortunately, he had gotten involved in AA, but what he learned there didn't always give him relief from his fears. He began to watch her movements in much the same way that she had watched his for so many years. Their dependence on each other was crippling. For a time it looked like their lives would unravel, but both of them realized that if they didn't make changes, their lives would unravel anyway. Carolyn credits the fact that neither of them left their recovery program for keeping their marriage intact.

As they grew in strength, individually and as a couple, another problem reared its ugly head. Their oldest son, Randy, became a heroin addict. All of the feelings and fear that Carolyn had had over Sam's drinking replayed themselves, only this time, she had tools she had not had before. She knew, in spite of what she occasionally thought, that she had not caused his disease, she could not control his disease, and she could not cure his disease. But she was devastated anyway. Sam was, too. He was also full of rage, the same way he had been when he had been drinking, and Carolyn began to feel the same anxiety, deep in her stomach, that she had felt in years past. Carolyn did what any serious Al-Anon person does. She doubled up on her meetings, going to as many as she could fit into her life.

The tools of Al-Anon continued to help her when her youngest son, Tim, also succumbed to addiction. For a time, when she first found out about Tim's addiction, she did get into a little case management. She thought that since she had been through addiction with Sam and Randy, she had some ideas on how to control his situation. Carolyn said it wasn't easy for her to understand the Second Step when she first read it, because she had never thought of herself as insane. Only now, as she faces another son's addiction, has she realized that most of her actions for years were indeed insane, and if she didn't have the program now, she would be insanely trying to manage Tim's drug use, his friends, his life, his dealer, his schooling.

Fortunately, when she began to struggle with Tim's situation, one of the first things she did was call her sponsor. Rona said, "Go to a meeting as soon as you can and call me back." Carolyn did. She said that when the group opened with the Serenity Prayer, she immediately felt a rush of peace wash over her. It was as though she had forgotten the most basic lesson of all: accepting what we cannot change, and changing what we can. She remembered that Tim had his own journey. It was not her journey. It was not Sam's journey. It was not Randy's journey. Tim had to find his own way, just as she had. The jury is still out on this situation. It is still out on Randy, too, in fact. He has found abstinence many times but has relapsed just as many.

▐▌█▌█▌█▌

LETTING THINGS REST

The miraculous thing is that Carolyn is serene most of the time. She knows she can't change anyone but herself. Letting others make whatever choices they feel compelled to make has gotten easier. None of the significant people in her life make the choices she might have made for them, but she can accept that now. The best part of this acceptance is that she no longer takes their choices personally. She learned from experience that you cannot detach when you are feeling responsible for someone else's behavior or taking their behavior personally. Either way you are a hostage.

Learning that she can survive a family crisis has been freeing. Carolyn has survived many of them now. She never waits for the other shoe to drop anymore. She knows that if or when something happens, her three decades of work will kick in, and she will move through the flood because she has learned to turn everyone over to God, who she knows will work things out for each person in the manner that is right for them.

Carolyn says one of her greatest joys is that she can "let things rest." In other words, she doesn't have to resolve every situation or conflict immediately anymore. I could relate to this joy when we talked. In my early recovery, not only did I make an issue of virtually every situation over which my significant other and I had differing opinions, but I also could not rest until we had come to an agreement, even if that meant I simply gave in. I was certain our disagreements meant he was considering leaving the relationship, and that terrified me.

Carolyn said that the best reward of sharing her recovery experience with Sam is that they are sharing a spiritual path, too. She had always hoped that would happen for them, but she had doubted for many years that it would. Even in the early years of recovery, they left this part of each other's program alone. Now they share prayer openly.

‖‖‖‖‖

INSIGHTS

When Carolyn's older son, Randy, became an addict, she knew she was powerless over the situation, but she also felt sick over their son's disease. Being a good Al-Anon student, she knew that shifting her focus away from her son would offer her some relief. She began to make that shift on a moment-by-moment basis. Whenever Randy's face or situation came to her mind, she replaced the thought with an image of her Higher Power.

Surprisingly, the visualization worked. Carolyn would get a moment's peace. Many times an hour she had to do this, but the effect was the same each time. She shared this technique with Sam, but he was not ready to give up his rage and try it.

Carolyn has continued to use this technique for a number of situations in her life over which she has no control. She says that this technique, along with the Twelve Steps and other Al-Anon principles, have offered her such an incredible breath of fresh air that she almost looks forward to being handed circumstances in which to use these tools. Each time she uses them, she feels empowered. No matter what problem she is facing, Carolyn has learned that the main thing she can really do is pray. She says she feels spirit filled most days, even when she wakes up. If the feeling isn't there, she gets on her knees and does the Third Step prayer: *God, I offer myself to thee—to build with me and to do with me as thou wilt. Relieve me of the bondage of self that I may better do thy will. Take away my difficulties, that victory over them may bear witness to those I would help of Thy power, the Love, and thy Way of Life. May I do thy will always.*

It always helps her remember who she is, who God is, and what the assignment for the day is. She knows her peace and serenity are dependent on her relationship with God, not with Sam, Randy, Tim, or anyone else. She also knows that praying might be helpful, so she does so quite willingly. The peace prayer offers her is almost as good as having everyone around her change, she says.

WORKING THE TWELVE STEPS: STEPS TEN TO TWELVE

STEP TEN: [We] continued to take personal inventory and when we were wrong promptly admitted it.

To stay on the recovery path requires certain commitments. One of the first is to do Step Ten on a regular basis. Most of us who have been making this journey for a while have made a practice of doing this step before retiring every evening. It doesn't have to be a formal undertaking. Even just a few, quiet moments of reflection about how the day just ending unfolded—what we liked about our behavior and what we know we need to address—must pass through our minds.

The work that needs to be done, the amends that need to be made, can be handled before they lead to unwanted judgments from others. The sooner we can clear the air, the easier our relationships will become. From my perspective, the primary benefit of the Al-Anon fellowship is healed relationships. Our relationships are guaranteed to be better, if not healed almost immediately, when we begin to take responsibility for actions that have affected another person adversely. Another advantage of doing a Step Ten every evening is that we can go to sleep with a clear conscience.

STEP ELEVEN: [We] sought through prayer and meditation to improve our conscious contact with God *as we understood Him*, **praying only for knowledge of His will for us and the power to carry that out.**

Besides doing Step Ten every night, it's helpful to experience Step Eleven, too.

I remember hearing at one of the first meetings I attended that praying was talking to God and meditating was listening to God's response. Listening to God is especially hard for codependents, I think, because our egos are constantly telling us what we need to be doing for others in order to keep them as happy hostages. And most of what we hear from this busy mind is not coming from God. But how can we tell the difference between the ego's voice and God's? That's the inevitable question.

If what we are hearing is unloving in any way, it has not come from God. If what we think we are being told to do is not an act of kindness toward ourselves or someone else, it did not come from God. The expression of love, and only that expression, is God in action. We will never be told by God to act in any way that is unloving.

Knowing what God wants us to do and then having the power to do that very thing is guaranteed if we both pray and meditate on a regular basis. Neither prayer nor meditation alone will be enough. Learning how to detach from the turmoil in our lives takes effort, and the effort is greatly helped when we pray and mediate as a matter of course every day.

If we turn over to God all that belongs to God—and everything belongs to God—and if we listen to the guidance that is then offered and willingly follow it, peace will be our reward. Our part in the equation may not sound difficult to everyone, but it generally sounds nearly impossible to codependents. We place our trust in everyone doing whatever needs to be done in the best way. Unless we can move beyond this perspective, we will not find peace.

STEP TWELVE: Having had a spiritual awakening as the result of these steps, we tried to carry this message to others, and to practice these principles in all our affairs.

This step is truly putting into action all we have learned in the rooms of Al-Anon. Modeling for others what it means to be on a spiritual journey and then living according to principles of honesty, honor, acceptance, trust, peace, and love are the very reasons we have "been selected by God" to share this message. Remember, there are no accidents. Our being *here, now* is intentional. Those traveling with us *here* and *now* are intentional participants, too. This step shows all of us a better way to be, a more peaceful way to live, and the freedom from obsession with others that we all deserve.

NOTHING LESS THAN FREEDOM

SHELLEY'S STORY

AUTHOR AND PSYCHOLOGIST VIRGINIA SATIR was quoted a number of years ago as saying that 98 percent of all families were dysfunctional. I am willing to believe that she was right. Shelley, like so many storytellers, used alcohol as one of the easiest ways to "slip away," thus not causing any upset in her ever-controlling family. This method worked for her throughout her twenties, and then the alcohol turned against her, as it is wont to do.

What she had discovered, though, in her pursuit of getting away, was that alcohol allowed her to close off her mind to what family members were doing and saying. She could "get away" rather than be always under their thumb. While drinking she was able to exist relatively unmoved by the emotional turmoil that was caused by their overinvolvement in each others' lives. We might not call this method healthy detachment, but for Shelley it was effective, nonetheless.

Shelley couldn't count on using alcohol when she was emotionally snagged by the behaviors of others in the workplace, however. At work, for instance, she needed to cooperate and find a middle ground when there was conflict. She also had to learn how to handle feelings of unworthiness when her ideas gained no favor with her colleagues. Alcohol simply could not be used as an escape in the workplace. Being able to forget her feelings with a drink in front of her fireplace at home after work was a far cry from learning how to detach, a tool to hone if she was to successfully handle everyday crises.

Shelley was able to enjoy her freedom in some settings but not all. She realized that she wanted to experience this freedom everywhere, but she also had the problem of alcohol to handle. It had imprisoned her, not unlike the way her family had imprisoned her. For so long alcohol had made her decisions for her, and she needed to take her mind back. She wasn't sure at first whether she knew how to think for herself.

Fortunately she sought the guidance of AA, and the others already gathered showed her how to traverse their path. Shelley is so grateful to AA for giving her back her decision-making ability, but she soon realized that AA didn't solve all of her people problems.

|◄|┉┉|►|

INSIGHTS

Shelley spoke lovingly of Ted, her significant other, and the "attachment" she had developed to him. She said when they first met, they spent long hours in conversation, detailing the experiences, past and present, of their lives. She was comfortable feeling attached to him because he inspired so many good feelings and she felt heard by him, a feeling she had seldom experienced before. He was present, honestly present, in their relationship. For Shelley, being attached is being *connected*.

Shelley says that for her, detachment first begins with that connected sense of attachment. Only then can she see the need she also has for separateness. Her feelings of connection were tested when Ted became very ill. She feared he would die and then felt afraid for her own life. When she realized she had these fears, she knew that her attachment had become unhealthy. Before the compulsion to worry overtook her, she had the strength to reach out to others, to seek the guidance of Al-Anon, and to use her mind to her advantage. She has become good at stopping her mind in mid-thought when the thought is not one that's beneficial to her.

Shelley has learned how to let people be themselves and take care of themselves. Even though Ted was ill and needed a lot of attention, she knew he also needed to begin doing things for himself. She let him. Even when he preferred that she'd take on his tasks, she left them to him.

Shelley has also learned that taking control of her emotions makes the difference between having a wonderful day every day of her life or being miserable. Not having her days in the control of someone else has miraculously changed her life, and it will change the life of everyone who practices detachment, she says.

CONCLUSION:
CHOOSING A NEW PERSPECTIVE

I WAS AT AN AL-ANON MEETING earlier today, and the topic was hope. There was a time in my life when I could not have imagined men and women sitting around for an hour discussing hope, because my own perspective on life was so devoid of hope. Now I am actually grateful that I was, at one time, hopeless. Had I not been so bereft of all hope, I would not have been willing to follow the suggestion of Toyce, a colleague, to go to Al-Anon.

I remember well her plea. I had been on a weekend binge, drinking in celebration of my birthday. She and I had dinner the previous night. When I got home that evening, an old friend was waiting for me, and we headed for one of the city lakes with a quart of rum and a liter of Coke. We sat there all night and all day (I think). I wandered home the following evening and fell asleep on the couch. When I awoke, I didn't know if it was dusk or dawn. I called Toyce to ask her, and she gasped, asking me what was wrong. In her worried voice, she said, "Karen, I think you'd better go to Al-Anon. The men you are hanging around with are drinking too much!"

I know now that Toyce didn't have the courage to tell me to go to AA, and I am certain I would not have received that suggestion very happily. But Al-Anon wasn't so threatening, and she wanted to help. I didn't immediately go, but I did consider it. Fortunately for me, Toyce repeated the suggestion a few more times. Finally, I promised her that I would go, and I was too ashamed not to keep the promise. I am certain that promise was the major turning point in my life.

After being in Al-Anon for a while, I ended up in AA, where I definitely needed to be, and exclusively, for a while. Then I went back to Al-Anon and have been in both programs ever since. My personal recovery has been doubly enhanced by this decision, one I think every other AA member should make.

All of us in any of the Al-Anon meetings rooms have a specific story that brought us there. Yet we all ended up there because we were meant to be there, and the people who have wandered across our paths have had divine appointments with us. I believe this absolutely, and it is what convinces me that the entire fellowship is God inspired. Each one of us has been called to do some very special work.

When I think of all that I have learned in Al-Anon, I am truly overwhelmed. It's true that I was initially introduced to the concept of detachment by reading Sidney Harris's explanation of why he was choosing politeness rather than nastiness in the book *Why Am I Afraid to Tell You Who I Am?* But it was the thousands of Al-Anon meetings I have attended over more than four decades that clarified the concept for me and made it mine.

Detachment truly is a gift, but it is often a misunderstood gift. It does not necessarily mean physically cutting ourselves off from people, although we may have to do that for brief periods. Rather, as the stories in this book show, detachment is a decision made in the mind and then held in the mind. We can detach our emotions from anyone anytime we decide to do so. The result is that we never become a hostage to someone else's behavior. Our freedom is guaranteed when we take charge of what's in our mind. This realization was astounding when I first heard it, and it continues to amaze me. I don't think anyone simply detaches once and permanently. I consider detaching to be a lot like brushing my teeth; it is a decision that needs to be made again and again.

In this book, the storytellers and I have tried to show that it is futile to try to control another person. If we had been successful at our attempts at controlling others, our lives would have been burdened forever. Our stories reveal the freedom that comes from letting others live their own lives. A mind obsessively filled with the actions of others, whether we deem those actions good or bad, is never going to be peaceful. On the other hand, a mind that is focused on a Higher Power and joy and hope will always be peaceful and miraculously helpful, in the right way, to the others on the path.

We have been gathered in the meeting rooms of Al-Anon because of our willingness to change and, in the process, to show others that change is possible. Our journey is not complete. But it will be as joyful, as hopeful, and as peaceful as we want it to be. All we have to do is keep showing up and continue to be willing to carry the message of love, acceptance, and faith to one another. Let's never forget that the greatest gift we can give another person is our rapt attention as our stories are shared. Honoring the spirit of God in them honors the spirit of God in ourselves, and the healing we all long for begins.

APPENDIX:
THE TWELVE STEPS OF AL-ANON (WHICH ARE BASED ON THE TWELVE STEPS OF AA)*

1. We admitted we were powerless over alcohol—that our lives had become unmanageable.

2. Came to believe that a Power greater than ourselves could restore us to sanity.

3. Made a decision to turn our will and our lives over to the care of God *as we understood Him.*

---

* The Twelve Steps of Al-Anon, as adapted by Al-Anon with permission of Alcoholics Anonymous World Services, Inc. ("AAWS"), are reprinted with permission of Al-Anon and AAWS The Twelve Steps of Alcoholics Anonymous, AAWS' permission to reprint the Twelve Steps does not mean that AAWS has reviewed or approved the contents of this publication, or that AAWS necessarily agrees with the views expressed therein. Alcoholics Anonymous is a program of recovery from alcoholism *only*—use or permissible adaptation of AA's Twelve Steps in connection with programs and activities which are patterned after AA, but which address other problems, or in any other non-AA context, does not imply otherwise.

4.   Made a searching and fearless moral inventory of ourselves.

5.   Admitted to God, to ourselves, and to another human being the exact nature of our wrongs.

6.   Were entirely ready to have God remove all these defects of character.

7.   Humbly asked Him to remove our shortcomings.

8.   Made a list of all persons we had harmed, and became willing to make amends to them all.

9.   Made direct amends to such people wherever possible, except when to do so would injure them or others.

10. Continued to take personal inventory and when we were wrong promptly admitted it.

11. Sought through prayer and meditation to improve our conscious contact with God *as we understood Him*, praying only for knowledge of His will for us and the power to carry that out.

12. Having had a spiritual awakening as the result of these steps, we tried to carry this message to others, and to practice these principles in all our affairs.

ABOUT THE AUTHOR

K AREN CASEY, WINNER OF A 2007 Johnson Institute America Honors Recovery Award for her contributions to the field, is a sought-after speaker at recovery and spirituality conferences throughout the country. She has written nineteen books, among them *Each Day a New Beginning, It's Up to You,* and *Change Your Mind and Your Life Will Follow*—a bestselling book that is the basis for her Change Your Mind Workshops. In this book, Karen Casey focuses on codependence in a way that allows anyone who thinks they might be codependent—that is, living their lives according to someone else's idea of who they are and/or letting themselves unduly suffer the judgment of others and/or trying to control the behavior of others—in a warm, unique, and effective way.

Karen Casey divides her time between Minnesota and Florida. To learn more about her work, visit her at *www.womens-spirituality.com*

Mango Publishing, established in 2014, publishes an eclectic list of books by diverse authors—both new and established voices—on topics ranging from business, personal growth, women's empowerment, LGBTQ studies, health, and spirituality to history, popular culture, time management, decluttering, lifestyle, mental wellness, aging, and sustainable living. We were recently named 2019 and 2020's #1 fastest-growing independent publisher by *Publishers Weekly*. Our success is driven by our main goal, which is to publish high-quality books that will entertain readers as well as make a positive difference in their lives.

Our readers are our most important resource; we value your input, suggestions, and ideas. We'd love to hear from you—after all, we are publishing books for you!

Please stay in touch with us and follow us at:

Facebook: Mango Publishing
Twitter: @MangoPublishing
Instagram: @MangoPublishing
LinkedIn: Mango Publishing
Pinterest: Mango Publishing
Newsletter: mangopublishinggroup.com/newsletter

Join us on Mango's journey to reinvent publishing, one book at a time.